LANDSCAPES OF GLORY

Tom Davies, a Welshman born and bred, trained as a journalist with *The Western Mail* and later worked for *The Sunday Times*, *The Sunday Telegraph* and *The Observer*, where for three years he was the diarist Pendennis. Now a full-time writer, he has written ten books and his *Merlyn the Magician & the Pacific Coast Highway* was short-listed for the Thomas Cook Travel Book of the Year Award, while his pilgrimage narrative *Stained Glass Hours* won the Winifred Mary Stanford prize for the best book with a religious theme. He lives in Penarth in South Wales and is married with three sons.

Landscapes of Glory
AN ENGLISH PILGRIMAGE

Tom Davies

TRIANGLE

First published in Great Britain in 1996
Triangle
SPCK
Holy Trinity Church
Marylebone Road
London NW1 4DU

British Library Cataloguing-in-Publication Data
A catalogue record of this book is available from
the British Library

ISBN 0–281–04908–4

Typeset by Dorwyn Ltd, Rowlands Castle, Hants
Printed in Great Britain by BPC Paperbacks Ltd.

Illustrations by
Jean Freer

Contents

Foreword

There is an ancient, celestial myth which I recently made up and it goes like this – If you took a Scotsman, an Irishman, a Welshman and an Englishman into the great cathedral of Heaven, full of high, sloping wonder, the reaction would be thus:

> The Scotsman would marvel at the architectural form, and respectfully design additional adornments. The Irishman would glow a rich smile and compose a lyrical poem. The Welshman would weep in other world tongues, and then sing a vast, rolling hymn. As for the Englishman, he would mutter, 'very nice', and start playing with the fluff in his anorak pocket.

The resurgence in recent years of Celtic and Ancient Briton spirituality has seen the prayer-book English somewhat left behind in the choir stalls, perhaps still disapproving of the passionate tribes of Caledonia, Hibernia and Gwalia.

Tom Davies, Welshman and contrary pilgrim has, through *Landscapes of Glory*, issued a generous invitation to the English to come and sup anew from the rich chalice of their divine history as he takes the reader on a contemplative trek from Cornwall in the south-west to Lindisfarne in the north-east. What with his ceaseless travels from old shrine to even older mountain-top, he has probably become our only professional pilgrim.

Anything that Tom Davies writes will contain the best attributes of the poetic, questioning soul – compassion, awkwardness, child-like wonder, a love of the absurd, devout anarchy, a loathing of the trite, and a necessary realization that repentance, for many, is a complex and highly individual process. And what's more, it's such a long, long way to Calvary from anywhere. Well it is if you are serious about the journey, although the view is beyond breath when you get there.

Tom's affection, and yearning, for the wayward English to take sanctuary once again in the light and shade of the ageless, brooding God shines out from this precious and diligent book. Along the way you'll observe the sincere, sober and occasionally barmy ways the English have attempted to attain some sort of harmony with the tender parent and unknowable conundrum that is, was and will be God. From caved-in monasteries to hermit prayer cells, from the summer lanes of Gloucestershire to the autumn glaze of Northumberland, the walk is rich, entertaining and inspirational. The book is worth buying alone for Tom's meditations on the bees of Buckfast Abbey.

St Cuthbert, with whom the reader is left at journey's end, observed the dying days of his spiritual master, the Venerable Bede, and noted that during one of the old cleric's prayers when he came to the incantation 'Do not leave us orphans', the Bede 'wept copiously', causing Cuthbert and other novices to do likewise; this lamentation carrying on later into their study periods.

If it is possible for a Welshman to intercede on behalf of the seared soul of the English, then part of Tom Davies' prayer that is *Landscapes of Glory* is for the easterly neighbour, pleading at the deep door of Paradise, 'Do not leave us orphans, do not leave us orphans'. A universal petition for us all in these fractured times.

Stewart Henderson

ONE

Secret Places of Prayer

TO START A summer pilgrimage through England where better than on her most southerly tip, the Lizard, in Cornwall, cruising the lanes and lay-bys and wandering across beaches and past coves, watching the ancient and ceaseless battle of wind and wave or else kneeling in prayer in an empty, stone chapel and hearing again a storm hammering on the old slate roof as the congregation sings 'For Those In Peril At Sea' driven on by the fat, breathy blasts of the harmonium?

What could be better than standing here with warm winds playing on your cheeks and listening to the frequent and loud ancestral voices in these summer lanes? The hedgerows are hives of ceaseless activity just now, bursting with flowers which keep blooming their brains out for week after week since the winters are mild down here and there are no frosts, with bees diligently going about their bee business, zooming in and out of the mouths of each small flower as cabbage whites tumble this way and that in huge wheels of fermenting sunshine. Just down there, half-buried in some spiky brambles, is an old water pump.

Almost every foot of every hedgerow is a tiny miracle of wonder with pink bursts of campion or lurid wafts of bluebell scent. Clumps of foxgloves rise up over the gorse and black-thorn. The outlying fields are strewn with ancient rocks lying around in ancient postures and, occasionally, if you are lucky, you will chance across some rackety kissing gate or long-forgotten plague stone.

Every few yards there will also be some spry sparrow or de-mented starling setting the hedgerow alight with their whistling happiness. But what I want to know is why are these birds so happy all the time? Why don't they ever get depressed like everyone else? When did you last hear a bird complaining about its gout or a bad night's sleep or how the bank manager was on his tail yet again. All they ever do is whistle all day long without ever getting puffed or whistled out. They're at it morning, noon

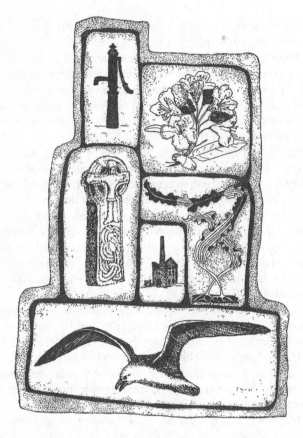

and night – no matter if there's some new disease sweeping the land or the economy has gone bust yet again – all of them, every single one of them, busy whistling their little heads off in each and every hedgerow as if their lungs were permanently engaged in some endless celebration of a recent victory at war or a birthday without end.

There are always exceptions, of course, like that pair of magpies marauding around near that stile. There's nothing more awful than magpies who rob nests and eat the young; they're forever brawling with other birds too; they pinch things and can't even whistle properly, settling for a sort of aggrieved clinking.

I was staying at Trelowarren, a retreat centre in a huge old country house in the heart of the Lizard, thinking such thoughts about them I loves and them I hates in the bird world and strolling around the vast grounds, when their various whistles began to die away since the night was now beginning to reclaim the day. Everywhere in the grounds there were Himalayan ranges of rhododendron bushes and, this late, everything was quiet except for the low buzzing of hundreds of bees working each and every rhododendron flower. A rabbit stuck its head out of a hole and looked at me. Far away the sound of a speeding car. Trelowarren House itself looked like a castle which had been involved in a nasty collision with a chapel which was full of Pontypridd Baptists last week. This week there was just one pilgrim here – me.

But now with the darkness thickening above the old house it did not take too much of a leap of the pilgrim imagination to re-create the older times when the dark shapes of Neolithic men stumbled through those woods and over those fields, dragging their huge stones to build their jumbled pyramids in praise of their gods or else quietly skinning an animal or communicating Neolithic thoughts to one another through smoke and fire. It was all darkness and pagan fire around here then as flints struck together in streams of sparks and the evening sky was lit by nothing brighter or more technological than stammering revelations of lightning.

But today when the pilgrim eyes lift above the flatlands of the Lizard they see not the works of Neolithic men but lines of wind farms with propellor blades stuck to poles like eternally struggling moths; they will see hovering helicopters from the nearby RAF station but, even more amazingly, they will also see the

3

moon-faced satellite dishes of Goonhilly Research Station, all nineteen of them busy sending television pictures all over the world while also handling thousands of phone calls, air phone calls, faxes and telexes.

Goonhilly is at the very forefront of the modern world and, looking around it, you begin to sense the process by which we once spoke to one another with fire but then went on to use semaphore, radio, radar and now this, a centre for a million messages concerning small and big dramas, the biggest earth station in the world. Fire has long become redundant since we now listen instead to the signals from metal balls revolving the earth 22,000 miles up in the sky.

Yet even amongst all this high-technology Mother Nature remains defiant since you can still find the rare Fragrant Orchid and the Hairy Buttercup here. Adders still bask in the sunshine near the dishes and two kestrels actually nest in Aerial No. 2 which also transmitted the Live Aid concert to two billion people throughout the world.

Just next to that dish is the Dry Tree Standing Stone, erected by Neolithic men and standing there still, in motionless and stricken testimony to our failures to communicate with each other and, even more ominously, with God.

The most difficult part of any book is actually getting it started. How to find that one line or that blazing paragraph of truth which will seize the attention like a punch on the nose and then keep hold of said nose for the following hundred pages or so? I had been thinking a lot about that opening paragraph in those ravishing Cornish lanes; about how I could open my pilgrimage through England with an explosion of drama and words which would launch my narrative off the starting blocks without once pausing for breath or a look sideways for the whole long sprint straight down to the finishing line of the last page. And then I got it.

I was in a hidden grove of tangled oaks when a huge tiger came bounding towards me. There were lions too and wolves, none of them particularly ferocious but not terribly friendly either except that they were all luminous. *Luminous!* They were all glowing and with some strange internal light which gave their stripes, mane and teeth a singular menace. And now they were coming for me, about to sink half a dozen sets of their luminous fangs right into me. Me!

But even in such extreme peril; even with every limb about to be forcibly ripped from one another, all I could hear was this writerly voice, *my voice*, shouting: 'Well doesn't this beat all? Isn't this the greatest moment with which to start what will surely be the greatest book ever written about any pilgrimage anywhere? Geoffrey Chaucer eat your heart out.'

Then I woke up in my lonely room in Trelowarren with nothing, fanged, luminous or otherwise, about to tear me apart. It had been a dream and in those awful moments of total lucidity that often follow a lively dream I remembered that I had gone with my family a few weeks earlier and we had all sat in the safety of a car watching the lions sleep out in the grass at Longleat House. How easily and readily our sleeping imaginations transform tranquil reality into ferocious nightmare.

I wandered out on to the landing of the house and made myself a cup of totally untroubled tea, staring at the wall while the kettle boiled and then, unable to find any milk, having to drink it black.

The next morning I plunged on again, past old arsenic mines and the ivy-throttled skeletons of dead Cornish beam engines, until I hit the foxgloved lane to Zennor along the north coast. The air was swarming with sunshine loveliness and there was a power and grandeur about that coastline that kept making me want to crash to my knees and bow my head.

D. H. Lawrence once wrote that when he looked down on Zennor he knew that it was The Promised Land and that a new heaven and earth would take place. But he was to change his tune about The Promised Land since the locals suspected him and his wife of sending signals to Nazi U-Boats and duly flung them out on their ears.

Virginia Woolf was to find her early literary imagination trapped by the savage sweeps of this Cornish coastline too. There were all those white Cornish cottages poised on cliff edges staring out at the Scilly Isles and Gunard's Head. Then there were the lamenting gulls and the tenacious limpets; the brackish seaweed and the roar of waves smashing against the rocks. These Cornish landscapes – the very music of Cornwall – were orchestrated, albeit in different guises, throughout the body of her later work even when it was set in the Hebrides.

But not everyone loved this place. John Heath-Stubbs wrote: 'This is a hideous and wicked country, sloping to hateful sunsets and the end of time.'

I liked Zennor a lot, enjoying The Wayside Museum immensely and warming to the scattered houses and gardens with their fantastic palms and tropical plants. The small granite church was delightful too. Almost as soon as you stepped into it you felt it was still alive with long years of love and faithful prayer.

This church would have been one of the first outposts of the Age of the Saints in the sixth and seventh centuries and it still looks pretty amazing today with its Cornish barrel-vaulted ceiling made in the style of a ship's keel. There is a sun dial outside too and two pairs of crossed bones telling us that our time always ends in death. 'All that pass by pray cast an eye,' it says on one of the tombstones. 'As you are now so once was I.'

In the side chapel is a chair and a love story which can still bring a tear to the eye and a sniff to the nose.

A beautiful young woman in the congregation was a devoted fan of the singing of a chorister Matthew Trewhella, the story begins. She loved to listen to his singing and one evening managed to entice him down into a stream and thence to a nearby cove where they disappeared forever.

On a warm and still evening you can still stand on that headland and hear a number of things. You can hear the waves breaking on the rocks. You can hear the blood moving through your ears and, if you are very lucky, you can hear the mermaid and the chorister still singing their love songs to one another.

Many years later a sea captain anchored his ship just off the coast when a mermaid bobbed up and asked him to park his ship somewhere else. Why *ma chérie*? Well he had parked over the entrance to their cave thus stopping her and her family getting in and out. Ah, so that's where they ended up.

It is a fine story which even comes with a happy ending and

that chair in the chapel is called The Mermaid Chair in honour of her. In the Middle Ages the symbol of the mermaid was used to teach people about the two natures of Christ – the human and the divine. In fact most of the symbolism of the Early Church came from the sea which is why in old churches we keep finding so many carvings of dolphins, whales, fish and even merrymaids as the Cornish fishermen used to call them.

But it has to be said that there's barely a rock or cave around here that it is not overlaid with some unlikely story or other. Every mine has its knockers and nuggies or creatures living in limbo whom the miners should never upset by whistling while they worked. There are fish that choke little children to death and stories of pirates so evil that even their fellow pirates threw them overboard. Rocks howl prophecies or develop mysterious holy scars. There are houses especially built for giants and nasty witches who have died beneath big, black clouds. The Cornish have been making up these stories for years and there's no sign of a ceasefire just yet.

As I travelled on through Cornwall, past extinct tin mine and golden estuary, I kept picking up echoes of the land's history, those fabled places where rebellious silver miners were thrown into a pit to cool off; where children were shut inside lime kilns to cure them of whooping cough; where tin miners were blinded by crude blasting methods, tar was burned in the streets to ward off cholera, and dense fogs hung in the air as the very land hummed in the flame and flood of an industrial revolution.

In 1880 the area was producing enough arsenic to kill every man, woman and child in the world. This arsenic was being used to fight the boll weevil in the American cotton crop and, while it was being refined, the sulphur closed down the schools, decimated the surrounding land and made cows sag to their knees and roll over dead.

This huge industry of death and poison has now long gone leaving a haunted landscape of strawberry fields and plunging waterfall. Everywhere you look there are ghost villages and deserted quarries and, deep down in a lane near Redruth, I discovered a genuine and moving spiritual oddity: an old mine which had been transformed into a modern preaching pit.

You come across it suddenly and without warning after a sharp bend in the hedgerows. There is a small white chapel and you walk up a hill past it coming out into a sort of Roman amphitheatre with huge grassed circles rising up to a surrounding wall. Listen quietly to any movements in the air since some of the greatest gladiators of the pulpit have addressed thousands in this, Gwennap Pit, built by tin miners who cleared the old pit before carving out this amphitheatre in the earth.

It was on that very spot that John Wesley began pounding out the soul of Methodism followed by various other preachers who assailed 'the pomps and vanities of this wicked world'. See those crowds coming down those lanes again in large omnibuses and on humble donkey carts, moving past dozens of blind men and beggars 'making their dolorous appeals to the passing throngs', past the gingerbread and cake stalls, the ladies in their holiday dresses and carrying parasols, the men in their top coats and fob watches on their waistcoated bellies, all come to hear a dying man preaching as to dying men. 'I shall never see a larger congregation until we meet again in the air,' Wesley wrote in his journal.

And they've been coming here ever since – the Oddfellows, Foresters, Philanthropists and Rechabites, the Methodists, the Baptists, the Congregationalists, the Salvation Army, the Torbay Gospelaires – all of them gathering, come rain or shine, in the high, grassed circles of this preaching pit to listen to God's holy requirement that his people be holy too.

When I took on this book part of my brief was also to try and report on the spiritual state of England. This task is probably impossible but it was while digging around in another Cornish village that I came across a strangely inspiring and compelling story.

A Lancashire couple had taken over an old school there and converted it into a pretty and bright chapel with its own baptistry. They told me over a meal how the Lord had called them to move down from the North to set up 'a house of quiet and healing' here in Cornwall. They had done this completely by faith, first stumbling across this virtually derelict school and even bidding for it at auction without actually knowing how or if they were going to get the money to complete the deal on time since they had not yet sold their own house. 'Don't give up,' God kept telling them. 'Put the fleece out again.'

The money finally did arrive within an hour of when it was needed and, during the long renovations, the money remained so tight that they often had to stand in the street and decide if they were going to buy a loaf of bread or a lavatory roll. But they managed it in the end after years of struggle – and oh, what a lovely, uplifting place it is, used by many of the local churches for meetings, retreats or quiet days. 'The sun of righteousness shall rise with healing in its wings,' it said on one of the walls.

I wanted to write their story and they readily agreed but a few days later the man in question rang me and explained that the Lord had spoken to his wife saying that their centre should remain a secret place so, of course, I couldn't identify its name or location.

But I then began to wonder if their story might somehow be a key to an understanding to the spiritual state of modern England. We had all agreed over that meal that we were worried about our children and that we were moving towards end times of lawlessness and a demoralized Church.

So could it be, I went on to wonder, that the Lord was busy setting up secret places of prayer all through the land? Could it be that he was in fact busy making preparatory moves for the end times? These were tremendously exciting questions and only a lot more travelling down a lot more English country lanes would see if I could come up with anything by the way of any exciting answers.

TWO

An Escape from Dartmoor

A LONG SUMMER day in Buckfast Abbey – rather like every other long summer day there – began with a peal of bells and a perfect sunshine stillness on the outlying lawns. The church itself was still dark with a single light being turned on in the choir stalls and two candles lit on the altar. Two lines of monks came filing into the stalls, taking off the hoods of their habits as they approached. There was a soft knock on wood. 'Hide me in the shadow of your wings from the violent attack of the wicked.' Another day of worship and work in Buckfast had begun.

This was the Morning Office – a mixture of devotions and chanted psalms – and you reflected on how little the voices or style of these monks can have changed since the monastery was founded in 1018. The collective voice was masculine and strong with a hint of abject melancholy. Even as they continued singing the swelling sunshine was gathering warmly and brightly in the purples and mauves of the stained glass above the altar. Other windows were also brightening with a faint golden fire. 'He will give light to those in darkness and those who dwell in the shadow of death.'

Breakfast consisted of a silent Weetabix and a thoughtful cup of tea. All meals here are taken in silence – apart from a reading at the evening meal – and we retreatants managed to communicate our wants with looks and fingers poked at such as the marmalade.

This lot could have been as rum a bunch of retreatants as had ever gathered under any abbey roof: two bee keepers from Germany; a man who had been touring monasteries for two years trying to decide if he was going to become a Roman Catholic; a Dublin teacher licking his wounds after a collapsed marriage; a man who had been making a film about the monastery for years but didn't seem to have a camera, and one who only put his teeth in when drinking but took them out again when he sat down to eat. When we weren't having our meals or sitting

together in a service we sat together in the common room and argued about everything under the sun. But it was surprising how quickly and easily even our fairly anarchic bunch fell into the monastic routine which in many ways has more rules than a council swimming pool: no talking here, no walking there, keep off the grass, door closed at 9.15 in the evening.

There was another peal of bells and Mass followed breakfast with a reading by a tiny nun and the haunting sound of Gregorian chant for the psalms. After Mass the full working day began and I tagged along behind the bee keepers since they had told me that today was a red letter day in the bee calendar. Today they expected the queen bees to fly out of their hives for the first time when they would mate with about half a dozen drones for about two and a half minutes each, whereupon the drones would fall dead to the ground and the queens would return to the hive and begin the long process of producing lots of little bees.

(I liked the two and a half minute touch and could somehow see the two of them running beneath the mating bees with stop watches in their hands.)

It all sounded simple enough except that, after a long and interesting conversation with Brother Daniel (one of the monks in charge of the bees) it turned out that, when it came to these monastic bees, there was nothing slightly simple about them.

Bees are a bundle of inherited instincts which they have handed down to one another for 50 million years, Brother Daniel explained. A lot of these instincts, like swarming, stinging children and dogs and not forgetting burglarizing weak neighbouring hives and making off with their honey, are nasty and anti-social so the Buckfast monks were now busy trying to sort them out and put these naughty bees back on the straight and narrow.

Each year they engineered some 500 virgin queens who were then carefully selected and bred so that they would be nicer, better-mannered and not gather in nasty threatening swarms. These bees would not attack children or dogs or go around thieving honey from the neighbouring hives.

Many hives are a riot of sex and violence which would do shame to the films of Quentin Cappuccino, it seems. Not only do they chase around the place in menacing gangs but they are even prone to attacking the queen bee and chucking her body out if she gets too old or boring. When they lose their queen the social order of the whole hive can then go to pot and anarchy rules.

But the good news was that the Buckfast monks were busy using genetic engineering to bring all this romping sex and violence under control. The Buckfast bee was going to be an extremely well-mannered bee; a by-word in polite civilization with none of the nasty aggression so characteristic of her sisters.

I must say the more I thought about it the more I loved the idea of a devout Benedictine bee; a sort of holy, loving bee who began the day with Gregorian chant and then worked hard around the clock without thieving from her neighbours or charging around in unruly gangs upsetting the horses or attacking little children. Indeed if there really was a way in which those monks could get the bees to attend a daily round of worship from Matins to Compline I was pretty sure that those clever monks would find it.

Time for lunch and, with it, the midday prayer in the chapter house. Visitors wandered in and out, some staying to join in and others staring in blank incomprehension as some monks took the lead and others chanted the response. They spend at least four hours a day in prayer and we quickly came to understand how prayer was the very foundation of the monastery. The monks perform their private offices too and there was so little public witness to almost all their acts of prayer that I had already begun wondering if perhaps Buckfast was yet another element in a great, secret tapestry of prayer which was being continually woven through the land.

But this sense of wonder always seemed to be hanging over everything for the modern pilgrim. Nothing was ever clear in this world and I often caught myself staring at the monks' faces and trying to guess what was going on in their minds. It was a totally redundant exercise, of course, and actually asking them rarely got you any closer either. A lot of them actively dislike any strangers' questions particularly if this stranger happens to have a pen and notebook in his hand. Groups of monks have taken one look at my notebook and taken off with their heads bowed and elbows flapping up and down with fear as if I had been wielding a shotgun.

These monks had fine faces though, each as vivid as a Rembrandt with their own bearing and personality. Many were old and gnarled but a surprising number had the sparkiness and unrealistic hope of youth. Most of the laughter lines had gone though; each was careful in his holy and devoted obedience.

Lunch was soup and steak-and-kidney pie with jugs of cloudy beer brewed with the standard Boots home brew kit. It was sturdy fare with everyone gobbling it down so fast it suggested that a famine was about to break out. The abbey takes no hard line on the consumption of alcohol and indeed brews its own tonic wine which is so strong that it is best drunk while already lying down. After coffee and a break in the calefactory – so-named because it was once the only place with a fire – the monks streamed back to their various tasks again: running the bookshop, the cafeteria, the gift shop, the brewery or making stained glass.

They have found that they need to run these commercial operations to keep going but they always seemed to get mysterious and even defensive if ever I raised the question of money. But it was one of my fellow retreatants who finally revealed all or, at least, put everything in perspective.

There were just four things that even God himself didn't know, he explained in all earnestness. God never knew what a Jesuit was thinking. Furthermore God didn't have a clue how many female orders were in the Roman Catholic Church nor could he ever foretell what a Franciscan was going to do next. God also, it seemed, didn't have the slightest idea where Benedictines got their money.

Supper was another solid wodge of food during which one of the monks read an extract from Lawrence Durrell's *The Greek Islands*. I had an odd feeling just sitting there in silence trying to eat and listen to Durrell's overwrought prose at the same time. Durrell was describing, with a detached amusement, some of the characters that he had met on Mykonos. I remember that I had once been considerably amused when, as a journalist, I had met him many years ago. From his books I had formed the impression of a tall, excessively handsome man who probably went everywhere dressed in a black cloak with a rose in his teeth.

But when I finally did meet him, in a bookshop, I was introduced to almost the tiniest man I had ever seen outside a circus ring. He was carrying a string bag full of groceries and was almost as bald as a billiard ball. He not so much spoke as squeaked in irritated chirps about some publisher who had upset him. In my view writers should always stay hidden away and let their books do all the talking.

Compline – that small and dark service of chanting and shadows which marks the end of the monastic day – was perfect in its serenity and simplicity. This is the time when all the nameless terrors of the coming night are fully and finally exorcized; this is the time when the monks say their goodnight prayers to God while moving around a single guttering candle which holds their prayers.

Their voices carried strongly in the warm evening air and you just knew that God was right there listening intently to the prayer and praise he so loves to hear in much the same way as he once listened to St Benedict with all his monks in Monte Cassino.

Yet more bells marked the end of Compline and the start of The Great Night Silence in which you could lie abed and really hear nothing but silence as all those monks dreamed of whatever monks dream about, if indeed they have energy for the luxury of a few harmless dreams after their long day's labours tending gardens, making stained glass or evangelizing bees.

Certainly the monastery lent itself to deep, untroubled sleep and almost the last image in my mind before I dropped off was of a huge wing of an angel stretching out of the darkness and enfolding the whole building, which would then be held in complete security and safety until the coming dawn.

Perhaps it's all to do with the great size of Dartmoor or perhaps it's something to do with that huge granite prison in Princetown but there is certainly a disturbing and unsettling presence about The Moor. On my pilgrimage across it my imagination kept dislocating and I was always thinking of myself as someone else – as a rich merchant perhaps, astride a horse and setting out for Canterbury, or even a mendicant friar with a bell and a thirst for lots of beer.

It was while walking along the Abbott's Way to cross the southern part of The Moor from Cross Furzes to Tavistock that I kept thinking of myself as a prisoner escaping that 'purgatory of lost, forgotten lonely and tormented souls' in Princetown. The more I thought about it the more real my situation became until I began all but galloping past the old stone crosses, high tors and long-forgotten tombs in my anxiety to get to the safety of Tavistock.

The howling of pursuing bloodhounds played in my ears and, at one stage, I was even cowering a bit with an arm raised over my head as a helicopter swooped low and I caught sight of the small face of the pilot looking down at me. No sooner had he gone than the bayings of those infernal bloodhounds began again.

But after rotting for so long in my small, airless cell I wasn't going to give myself up now so I struck out again for the wide open spaces of The Moor where the sunshine and high winds were busy singing endless songs of freedom. I scrambled past grazing horses and the eyes of watchful rabbits. I leaped streams and dashed past standing stones whose picked eyes watched my escape too. I began running along the length of one stream – as I had once seen Paul Newman do in some escape film or other to put the dogs off my track – and, just near Vixen Tor, I had to stop and rest, curling up on the ground beneath a bush with my trousers soaking and listening only to the frightened pounding of my heart.

Someone once described Dartmoor as the fatherland of rains from mist to waterspout but today – the day of my escape – the blue sky was full of drifting clouds and sunshine moving around in shifting pillars of glory. With such clear visibility it wouldn't be advisable to stay put for too long, particularly now some crows were fluttering down around me, doubtless interested in my sandwich and wanting to share it. You can always tell a crow because he walks around with his chest puffed up like a policeman. Rooks hop all over the place.

There were plenty of other animals out here . . . sheep, ponies, cows . . . all managing to keep the grass down to golf-course length. On the far side of The Moor the pillars of sunshine caught in the windscreens of passing cars and, over on my left, there was some sort of radar screen which was doubtless trying to track me down too. I could just see the pictures on television now – of the tied sheets hanging out of my cell window and then the broadcast warnings about a dangerous Welsh pilgrim out on the run. 'He is armed and dangerous and should not in any circumstances be approached by any member of the public.'

A breeze carried yet more noises of baying bloodhounds and I was up and off again, running along streams, ducking down past burial chambers and stopping to take cover behind a lone stone cross to take a careful look back and see how far they were away. But even out here in this huge wilderness and with the cover of this stone cross it would be difficult to escape them for long. They'd surely get me in the end and fling me back into that hated cell where I would cry and pound the metal door with the hams of my angry fists, stormily protesting my innocence.

I ran from rock to rock before clambering breathlessly to the top of the next high hill. And there it was all around me again – the great and thrilling range of The Moor, many of the hills nippled by high rocks and vast tanks of sunshine rumbling slowly and luminously from one valley to the next.

Then it happened; that strange moment of epiphany that is well-known to all pilgrims: a pilgrim moment of final release when all your pursuers have given up and gone home and you are left just standing there with your eyes closed, holding your face up to the sun with nothing but a celestial blaze in your brain as you know – you just know – that you are standing close to the perfect stillness and balance of Christ; that you are feeling the presence and protection of a steadfast love and that you are not being pursued by bloodhounds at all but protected now and for all time as you just stand there on The Moor with your heart beating softly in perfect time with the vastly greater and all-protecting heart of God.

The next day, wandering through another afternoon of clear sunshine, it rose up over me like a rather unlikely lighthouse that had been placed, as if by some vast accident, in the middle of dry land. This was St Michael's Church on the Rock at Brentor, perched precariously on the top of an extinct volcano. 'A church, full bleak and weather beaten all alone, as if it were forsaken,' Tristram Risdon wrote in 1625. 'Whose churchyard doth hardly afford depth of earth to bury the dead; yet doubtless they rest there as in sumptuous St Peter's, until the day of doom.'

The church retains a congregation of around twenty for her Sunday services in the summer months and they must rank as one of the fittest gang of worshippers in any parish in the land since I found the climb to the porch on about the same level of difficulty as scaling the South Face of Annapurna. 'Where's the oxygen mask then?' I asked one old woman who laughed loudly. 'I do this every day,' she snorted. 'Nothing in it.'

The labourers who first built this stone eerie in the high winds, which also overlooks much of Devon and Cornwall, can't have had much fun either. In fact I was pleased to learn that all they did was moan and groan as they hauled their rocks up here. 'A late curate at Tavistock who took services at Brentor and often found it desperate work to scramble to the summit in storm and sleet and rain resolved on forming a roadway,' it said in *The Book of Dartmoor* (1900).

> He experienced some difficulty in persuading men to go out from Tavistock, so he supplied himself with several bottles of whiskey and when he saw a sturdy labourer standing idle in the market place he invited him into his lodgings and plied him with hot grog till the man in a moist and smiling condition assented to the proposition that he give a day to the Brentor path.

At one burial they all came out of the church door only to be all but flattened by the unruly blasts of north-west winds. The only answer was for them all to proceed towards the grave 'crouching down like frogs' finishing the service by taking shelter behind the other headstones.

On the day I called they were fixing the spire, which had been struck by lightning, and the builder said he had to bring up a sack of lime in a barrow and had to stop for breath about ten times.

But it is a fine, fit building. 'Other men have laboured and ye have entered into their labourers,' it said on the wall inside. Yet there was something about this church high on a rock that kept reminding me of another church high on a rock I had once visited. They had the same names too, I recalled, when my memory took me by the hand, taking me to that distant place and setting me down in it: Skellig Michael, yet another holy place named after the archangel Michael.

This church was in fact a monastic ruin set out on an island in the swells of the Atlantic off the west coast of Ireland. There was an old stone oratory and six beehive-shaped stone huts, lots of weather-scarred crosses and a slightly bathetic graveyard, no bigger than a small flowerbed where the old monks had long been buried beneath the ground and continual swirl of thousands of gannets.

Even here in Brentor I could reach out and touch those tiny gravestones on the Skelligs. Both places were separate but as one. Both had been inspired by the human need to find a place of worship far from the madding throng; both showed how holy men and women continually sought out the secrecy of the mountain, the island and the desert to slump to their knees in lonely quiet as they began yet another conversational prayer with God.

Indeed, a few days later I was on yet another journey to an even more distant place of pilgrimage as the MS *Oldenberg* chugged out of Bideford on a lumpy grey sea, heaving this way and that until Lundy Island finally hove into sight, a huge granite fist thrusting up out of the swelling waves. Banks of mist were pouring off the crown of the island as if it was some kind of giant stone kettle coming to the boil. So this was Lundy, home of puffins and star of weather forecasts, curator of Bristol Channel legends and adventure playground of dense fogs and wild winds. Some in Devon have called it the kingdom of heaven.

But it can be very foggy can this kingdom of heaven with visibility reduced to some six feet the time I was there, making me feel like some stumbling blind man moving around carefully lest I plunged straight over one of the high cliffs.

That afternoon I walked the length of the island with the air as warm as the tropics and alive with the warbling of skylarks and the distant crashing of the waves. Deer, horses and wild goats emerged from the swirling mists. A few crows flapped noisily overhead and, down on the seashore, there was the hissing noise of barnacles and the throaty calls of fat, lolling seals. There were lots of those puffins around too, the gaudy clowns of the seaworld who, I was told, will often stand around together in their holes in the ground and just talk to one another. They also fly out for sand eels for their young but seagulls often wait for their return and then pinch them out of their beaks. The gulls eat the puffins' young too. It's not a barrel of laughs being a puffin.

People also told me of other strange secrets of the island: of the sheep who thought it was a dog since it came running to you when you whistled, the wood pigeon addicted to cream crackers, the carp in the Rocket Pond who bit your fingers and the raven who flew around the place upside down.

The island had other heavenly attributes like the fact that there had never been any crime on Lundy. They did have a theft a few years ago but they caught the culprit immediately although it did make international news. The only telephone was always on the blink and there was no one saying 'Don't' or anyone saying 'Can't'.

A gap opened up in the mist near the church and the very air brightened with juggling balls of misty sunshine. But even so everything remained pretty indistinct and you were still hard pushed to make out where the sea joined the stone or if that really was a rat skittering across the sand so fast someone had just lit a match under its tail. The white surges of the waves did briefly become more visible – and hence noisier somehow – until the mists began moving on those juggling balls of sunshine again: hard-faced bank managers declaring that this wretched and unwelcome outbreak of fun just had to stop.

But there is a great soothing balm about this kingdom of heaven and when I left a few days later I sat on the aft deck of the *Oldenberg* and tried, but failed, to remember exactly what I had been worrying about when I had first arrived there.

A bearded old wino who had soiled his trousers was busy shouting the truth of his madness outside the front porch of Exeter Cathedral as I walked up through the precincts. They made a curious counterpoint: this incontinent old man who had long drunk his brains away, muttering nonsense about knives and policemen and his Uncle Bert. And there behind him this soaring stone creation with the distant sounds of choir practice and the occasional peal of the cathedral bells marking off the hours or calling on people to come in and get down on their knees.

And it is a lovely place inside too, full of space and lacy stonework, and I was fortunate to be taken around by a Dr Richard Taverner, one of those volunteer and inspired guides who can even make the tiniest and most disfigured lump of stone interesting. With a head shaped like a bald eagle's his fingers rose and dangled in the air as if he was playing an invisible piano as he took us through the building weaving a fantastic mythology of the ordinary and extraordinary.

Thus we were soon told why the font is always near the door since it symbolizes the entry into Christian life and over there was the tomb of the last man in Devon to die in a duel. This was the statue of a lady with two left feet, that was the room occupied by the dog-whipper and here was a memorial to a missionary killed by natives who were then smitten by remorse and sent the body wrapped up back to Exeter. This was the tomb of the forgetful bishop who rode everywhere on a yellow bicycle and sent a postcard to his wife: 'Am in Ilfracombe. Why?' Most of the sculptures were puns and there was supposed to be an elephant that had the back legs of a horse.

He made every corner of the building come alive. There was, you knew, nothing that he could possibly say that would be boring and an hour with him really did seem like five minutes.

But my summer pilgrimage had to move on. Over the border and into Somerset.

THREE

In the Court of King Arthur

WARM SUNSHINE GATHERED in the blackberried lane where the apples in the orchards were still small and green. The tarmac actually moved underfoot as if treading on some dead dog and you paused a lot in the lengthening shadows often thinking of something cold to drink.

A village began unfolding around me which was as pretty an English village as I have yet seen, with thatched cottages standing cheek by jowl and all looking down at me with their wildly improbable fringes and mullioned eyes. But it was the gardens which were the busiest hives of colourful profusion at this time of the year. Everywhere the flowers seemed to be actively competing with one another to be the brightest and gaudiest and smelliest on the block, with whole banks of hollyhocks standing in front of weeping willows and pendulous wisteria walls.

I would find the church up a hill and buried behind some trees, a window cleaner told me. A man was mowing the grass in the graveyard when I got there and a ginger cat was sitting on a wall, with its leg held aloft and licking its belly. Wood pigeons burbled and midges swarmed near a towering beech. The vicarage was a small and impossibly serene French chateau at the end of a long curving drive. But the vicar wasn't in when I called.

In the church porch there were notices asking if you were worried about a drink or drug problem. Are you disabled or ill? But then, stepping inside, there was that ravishing and enfolding coolness that all old churches seem to offer on hot summer afternoons. The sweat dried lightly in my hair and I took a pew to absorb the prayerful spirit of the place. There were a dozen or so bunches of lilies and carnations dotted around almost every corner and their scents mingled with that of wood polish. Light streamed through the stained-glass windows and down on to the altar. A lone fly was buzzing in the darkness near the font. On the far side two women were kneeling together in a small chantry taking one another through a prayer. There was plenty of

that here too: the unmistakable presence of whole lifetimes of believing prayer: difficult to describe but impossible to avoid.

Every church is special in its own way but this one has its own unique grandeur, particularly for anyone who cares for words, since we have come to the Parish Church of St Michael in East Coker and just behind me lay the ashes of Thomas Stearns Eliot, that Anglican with the pen of sublime fire. 'In my end is my beginning', it says on his epitaph. 'Pray for the repose of the soul of Thomas Stearns Eliot.'

And so, this hot summer afternoon in this beflowered shrine, I duly prayed for the repose of the old poet's soul, right next to his ashes and beneath three stained-glass windows depicting the figures of Faith, Hope and Love. That same fly was buzzing away in the darkness next to the font as I prayed that his soul was getting along without too much difficulty; that he was at peace and would still find time to come and watch over us less talented scribblers if only with the living example of his disciplined scholarship, the precision of his wordplay and that fantastic feeling and passion that he brought to everything he wrote. Most poets are but guttering candles when set against the sun of T. S. Eliot, I pointed out in my prayer. Only great writers like him are capable of saving us from our stupidity.

After I had finished praying for the peaceful repose of his soul I read the poem 'East Coker' which had been left there to be savoured again by the passing pilgrims, almost feeling the old poet's soul actually moving around inside me as those lines took me through 'the electric heat' and 'surly light' of those surrounding country lanes again before sailing on into a moving meditation on the cycles of life and the way in which we all move into the dark regardless of our status or class. It is also thought to be a celebration of an English tradition which will survive the betrayals of a contemporary generation.

An Andrew Eliot, a cordwainer, emigrated from East Coker to America in about 1650, settling in Salem where he was to become a member of the jury in the infamous Witch Trials. To his descendants Henry and Charlotte was born a son in 1888 in St Louis Missouri who was christened Thomas Stearns and later came to England. He liked it here so much he became naturalized and, in due course, became almost more English than the English. One of his last wishes was that his ashes should be put in the parish of his ancestors, here in East Coker. The stone was to say simply that he was A Poet and he was, he was.

Now the ashes attract pilgrims from all over the world and they have duly signed their names in the parish visitors' book with various comments which usually amount to 'Here at last!' Flicking over the pages of this visitors' book you could tell that the words of the Poet had probably been stirring in their minds for years and that old T. S. had probably got right inside them like some deadly virus at an early age and then kept gnawing away at their minds and thoughts with the long-standing discomfort that always seems to turn up hand in hand with long-standing truth.

'To me the proof of a man's goodness is his effect on others,' said W. H. Auden. 'So long as one was in Eliot's presence we felt it was impossible to say or do anything base.'

Later I left the Church and walked down the hill into the village of East Coker, stopping to talk to a man in his garden about the other villagers here; ex-diplomats, retired service personnel, builders, he said, all now living out the twilight of their lives in this gorgeous thatched place. 'But they're all feeling the pinch like everyone else,' he said, reminding me of another of T. S. Eliot's lovely phrases in 'East Coker' when he spoke of 'the ruined millionaires'.

The heat had lightened a shade now and the shadows were stretching out as I walked on down to the pub for a quick one. Swallows were flitting around looking for insects for their young, flying lower than usual and diving under the trees. Then, unusually for this time of year, because almost everyone was wearing sandals and shorts, I spotted a stooped old man dressed fastidiously in a jacket, tie and shirt, making his way towards me on the other side of the lane.

It could almost have been the Poet himself, making his way home for a little nap and another bout of quiet composition. The more the fancy took me the more real it became and I stopped to stare. It's him! It must be him! Now T. S. stopped and returned my audacious stare.

But not only was it not him, it didn't look anything at all like him. Just another of East Coker's ruined millionaires. But the beer in the pub was real enough even if it only succeeded in making me feel very tired.

The light was breaking up fast and the whole sky was sweating above the ruins of Glastonbury Abbey. Stumps of stone hovered unevenly over me is if they were the broken, grey teeth of some mouldering half-blind giant patiently awaiting the attention of some miracle dentist. Even this late in the afternoon, the stones were still holding on to the heat of a hot, still day.

The sounds of thunder kept rumbling distantly like the sharp loud cracks of furniture removal men. A magpie chattered in a short convulsion of agitation when everything fell silent again as the grey of the sky began curdling into an ominous black. The cracks of the furniture removal men became grander and more operatic. Then there was a long pause as if the men had gone away for a tea break only to return having found some cannon from somewhere, now busy firing shots at some invisible Armada. *Boom, boom. Boom, boom, boom.* The air got colder and a breeze sprang from nowhere. Cold rain spattered down for three or four seconds and stopped again. A grey squirrel was out foraging for something interesting to eat on the manicured lawns and a brilliant flash of light shot across the Tor behind me. *Boom, boom. Boom, boom.*

It was eerie being here alone in these marvellous abbey ruins watching the strange silhouette of the Tor framed by a flash of lightning. Those staying in the Abbey retreat house can wander the grounds at will and so, long after the last tourist had left on the last bus, I sat next to King Arthur's grave and tried asking him about the deep secrets of Camelot. More lightning and a further round of cannon. *Boom, boom.*

The Tor with its peculiar oblong tower set down on top of it seemed even more compelling this thundery day in July. Just walking up it that afternoon I again felt the presence of watchful angels that I always seemed to feel whenever I got near it. The whole area has an unmistakable spirituality which seems to come throbbing straight up out of the grassy slopes and you get a certain sense of somehow being enfolded in the lungs of God. The view up there is unrivalled too as you stare out over the Mendips, the Polden Hills and the Cheddar Gorge, all just sitting there waiting patiently and resignedly for the coming storm.

This town first began as a settlement, it is believed, way back in AD 63 when Joseph of Arimathea arrived here with a hundred and fifty disciples. He also, it was further reported, brought with him the chalice used in the Last Supper, the Holy Grail, a present from Pontius Pilate. Joseph put his staff down on Weary All Hill whereupon it immediately grew into a bush and burst into blossom. This became the Holy Thorn which grows here still and, believing that his arrival here was thus blessed, Joseph built the first Christian church of wattle and daub just about right on that spot there.

Joseph was said to have buried the Holy Grail in what became known as Chalice Hill which duly attracted a sundry gang of treasure-seekers, including the great King Arthur himself, all in search of the blessings and strength which came with the ownership of the Grail. The fabulous court of Camelot was said to be built near here and there was also the Isle of Apples – Avalon – where King Arthur was brought to die after his last great battle.

Today, whole areas of grass around the old abbey ruins were brown and crying out for the reviving kiss of rain. Already and so early in the summer there were circles of dead and brittle leaves around the trunks of the trees but, somehow, the promised storm couldn't seem to get going. It was all flashes and noises off. Distant voices mingled with children's laughter. A car engine started and the noise of a passing jet skewered swiftly and mechanically through the smouldering stillness of the gathering storm. *Boom, boom.*

Outside the abbey grounds in the streets of Glastonbury it is Babylon and there was much that would have made poor old T. S. Eliot break down and weep. I have been coming here on various obscure pilgrim endeavours for the last twenty years and there was always much evidence of New Age weirdness here but now this weirdness seemed to have become a major feature of the landscape. Skinheads wearing dog collars mingle with shuffling space cadets forever talking about their non-ideas in a nonlanguage. There are lectures on accessing your intuition with dowsing, devic contacts and all you need to know about astral sex and teabags. Almost all the shops seemed to be selling strange magical aromas, hand blended incense, polished mystic stones and any amount of twinkling gaudy rubbish which will conjure up a healing spirit or three.

You can hire a Miracles Room for £18 a night or have a revelatory Chakra reading with the international mystic clairvoyant Emma Howe. 'Heal present life problems and relationships with past life regression to realise your true life pathway and purpose. Accurate psychic readings and guidance. Colour Healing. Esoteric Astrology.'

They all doubtless came here attracted by cosmic aerials or ley lines or other holes in the head although I was pleased to meet the quite splendid Father John Ives with his long beard and the black robes of Orthodoxy. Father John left the Anglican Church in 1994 because he thought it was getting too vague and, instead of taking the usual step towards Rome, he embraced the British Orthodox Church instead, taking over an old chapel for services in Glastonbury and setting up his own shop here, The Orthodox Way, selling such as incense, charcoal drawings and triptychs handmade in Mount Athos in Greece. He didn't have to change any of his Anglo-Catholic beliefs when he made this step, he said, and felt called here to form a sort of island of sanity in the swirling seas of nuttiness all around. 'Glastonbury forms the important roots of the Celtic church and was a home for a great many of the Christian saints. We just couldn't hand it over.'

It was soon going to become dark and that storm was still trying but failing to burst through the coming night. It rumbled and moaned: it crashed and splintered but, no matter which way it turned, it couldn't quite break through.

I lay down on the grass next to King Arthur's grave and looked up at the overhanging ruins, trying to get my imagination to join up the outlines of the old working abbey, once said to be the largest in England and the very cradle of British Christianity. It was, in the words of William of Malmesbury, 'grandly constructed to entice the dullest mind to prayer' and all based on the Benedictine foundation of hard work and sacred learning.

The main figure associated with this abbey was St Dunstan who was abbot here in 940 and later became the Archbishop of Canterbury. He began organ playing in the church services and instituted bells to mark off the monastic hours and announce the start of services. He first came to live in a cell in Glastonbury and built up this abbey in a series of reconstructions. He also became the patron saint of goldsmiths, jewellers and locksmiths, once seizing the devil by the nose with a pair of tweezers, it was reported, and thus putting the devil's nose out of joint. One of his other little quirks was that he walked in his sleep long before anyone actually knew anything about sleepwalking.

The abbey was gutted by a great fire in 1184. 'What groans, what tears, what pains rose as they saw what happened and pondered over the loss they had suffered,' said one contemporary report.

> The confusion into which their relics were thrown, the loss of treasure, not only in gold and silver, but in stuffs and silks, in books and the rest of the ornaments of the church, must even provoke tears in those far away.

Two years after the fire the monks were said to have found the bodies of King Arthur and his queen in a hollowed trunk of an oak in the abbey grounds. This 'find' was nothing to do with the fact that the monks needed to find a lot of money to rebuild their abbey and so needed to beef up the pilgrim trade. Do you hear me? Nothing at all.

And so here I was now lying on my own in the darkness of this great ruin trying to hear those bells again and the romping notes of the great organ as those monks of old shuffled back and forth past me, dark on grey, all going about their monastic rounds. The bells stopped and Gregorian chant lifted in the sweating air. Those monks kept rearing up over me and through my body, muttering softly and darkly about that which had been lost and that which would be found again. The hem of one of their robes brushed against the back of my hand and I pulled it away sharply.

Ah yes, this was another of those pilgrim moments, connecting with the prayers and hopes of the past and realizing that I was but another tiny pipeline to a less than certain future. This abbey was once destroyed by fire so what was going to destroy us?

With such doomy thoughts I began sweating profusely and became almost at one with the sweating night. Those broken pillars towered over me again like threatening fists and those distant men began firing their cannon again. There was also another brilliant flash of lightning but I could tell that there was no chance that the storm was actually going to manage to break out of the night. This was going to be a struggle without end and those Glastonbury ghosts could come and kneel in prayer with me all night long in this hot, dry season but there was still not going to be any rain.

Most cathedrals have big, crunching personalities and a look of huffy hauteur which says: 'When I speak let no dog bark.' But there is a lightness and sprightly merriment about Wells Cathedral which always seems to act on me like a spiritual aspirin whenever I go near her.

She is a great buttressed beauty just sitting there in that most English of towns which always seem to be set out as invitingly as the tables of a huge banquet in the foothills of the Mendips. The front of the cathedral has several hundred sculptured figures, many of which were smashed by Cromwell's puritan rabble but are now undergoing renovation. Indeed the whole cathedral is said to be the repository of England's greatest collection of medieval sculpture and these vignettes in stone can teach us a lot about life in medieval England: a man repairing shoes, labourers working in the fields or boys pinching apples. There are no fewer than eleven sculptures of men suffering from toothache which perhaps tells us a lot about the hapless state of medieval dentistry.

The inside is pretty extraordinary too with huge strainer arches, like stone scissors, added to strengthen the building and giving the vague impression that this Gothic beauty has actually been furnished with a huge set of symmetrical stone ribs.

This was the first English cathedral conceived entirely in the Gothic style. I have always found it the most human and accessible of places, spending a lot of time pondering on the prayer requests. The range of demands which are continually being put before God is amazing. Many were pleas for cures for such as cancer in relatives but others were of the rather mundane variety like the fervent hope that God would help mean old Jack Smith to open up his wallet a bit more often.

But there is another small shrine here for the lighting of candles for loved ones and that also has long been a great favourite of mine, particularly with the printed explanation of the way candles carry our prayers long after we have finished them. I lit candles for my own loved ones and, if you gaze directly into the small fiery hearts of the flames for long enough, you can actually see their faces again, as smiling and as beautiful as they ever were.

Candles carry light into darkness. They offer up our prayers and the prayers of others. They remind us of those in history who have shone lights into the darkness. I am the light of the world, said the Lord.

Later I was having a cup of tea and a sandwich in a cafe when a man with a silver goatee beard and a healthy tan even though he was, I guess, seventy plus VAT, sat down at the same table. We chatted for a while and then, apropos of nothing, he began telling me a story about how he had been driving around the south of Spain. He had followed a sign saying SAFARI and had gone into this park where there were lots of lions basking in the sun. He had rolled down his window and actually roared at these lions because he was clearly a little odd and the lions duly got up out of their slumbers and stood there looking at him. An angry Spanish warden shooed him on and later in the car park he saw that the visitors' buses were covered with new bars.

He learned afterwards that the lions were newly arrived from Africa and had actually been attacking the buses and that it was not unknown for the lions to attack the cars too. For almost a year now he had been suffering from the same recurring dream that lions were hauling him out of his car and tearing his whole body apart bit by bit.

I kept thinking about his dream and my own dream of luminous lions for days afterwards; of how utterly human we all were, united by even the tiniest and most evanescent of events. We shared the land and the air and the sea. Some of us even believed in the same God but, when you really got down to it, we shared in one another's silly anxiety dreams too.

FOUR

The Death of a Monk

WITHIN A FEW weeks the summer sun had become merciless, rolling heat wave after heat wave over the countryside. The newspapers were full of stories about water shortages and hose-pipe bans and end-of-the-world talk about how it was the hottest and driest summer since, er, the last one. The Min. of Ag. was issuing press releases talking about 'moisture stress'.

All through the Cotswolds the harvest was at full swing with red puffs of poppies mingling in the golden corn. Some of the shorn, stubbled fields had huge bales of harvested straw lying around them like fat, chopped slices of golden Swiss rolls. This oxyacetylene heat had also turned many of the fields into scorched dust-bowls; it seared the very core of your being.

Cows kept bellowing for lack of sufficient water and pasture. The all-important grass fields for winter silage were barren and brown. This prolonged drought was also making the head of the corn small and stunted. Again the farmers were muttering about economic ruin. Nature gives a lot but, rather in the manner of a scorned lover, she can take away a lot too.

Ah yes, Nature had long found ways of blinding us with her radiance and suggesting to excitable poets that she was the very dwelling place of God – if not God himself – but, at the same time, she also had a way of quietly taking out a stiletto and plunging it into your blindly loving heart when you were not looking. And we began thinking about her again, wondering exactly *how* this occasionally ferocious and vengeful presence could be God who would do this.

There is probably not a farmer alive who is a pantheist or one who finds and worships God in nature. Certainly not any of the farmers in the Cotswolds this long, hot summer.

As I walked across those rock-hard fields around the Cots-wolds all I could see were jagged fissures in the parched earth and butterflies tumbling in the heat hazes. The fields should now be high with hay for winter feed but, even after being liberally

fertilized, they were covered in bald patches and such hay as there was had thin stalks and fat seed heads. The undergrowth was so sparse it would be difficult to harvest even that and, in the corn fields, convolvulus had wrapped multiple strangle-holds around the base of the stalks. Romping white carpets of May weed were spreading in all directions and there were vast holes in these carpets in which nothing at all, beneficent or malign, dared grow. Black holes in earth.

I had been staying with the monks in Prinknash (pronounced Prinage) Abbey in Gloucestershire, noticing that the local farmers had been moving the cows around a lot so that they could get the best out of each field. But there was precious little to munch anywhere and the cows, with swarms of flies bothering their big-lashed brown eyes, were bellowing their discontent long and loud. The farmers were reporting their milk yields well down on last year. Quite simply a cow does not stint on its own body if it is short of pasturing; it just produces less milk which, for an average farm, can mean as much as thirty gallons less each day.

Rabbits too – now largely immune to myxomatosis – had become unwelcome predators, forever chewing on the corn or what was left of the grass. 'I shoot them where possible but they disappear into the brambles where no amount of guns can get at them,' said one farmer with a sigh.

Practically the only ones without any complaint were the sheep who actually seemed to prefer the hot weather and foraging in the stunted dry grass. The heat also cut down on foot rot and parasites. After the harvest is over they will be put out in the stubble to graze in the weeds.

But it has to be said immediately that even this ferocious heat wave was causing no great problems to Brother Anthony as he toiled amidst whirling flights of ladybirds in the monastery garden of Prinknash. Everything was fine in this particular garden since this surprise swarm of ladybirds, possibly from Ireland, were gobbling up all the aphids and blackfly, which usually caused so much trouble, particularly to his beans, he said.

Let us pause for a moment right here while I sing you a hymn of love to the ladybird. Ladybirds are among the most enchanting and lovely members of the whole insect world, virtually without enemies of any kind except ants who, for some reason, will grab hold of them and chuck them around like a rugby ball. Ladybirds have a voracious appetite for just about anything a farmer or gardener dislikes and will devour aphids, scale insects, mealy bugs, thrips, caterpillars and mites. You name them and the ladybird will eat them. The more ladybirds in your garden the greater it will grow. The more ladybirds we have the less spraying we have to do.

The lady and gentleman ladybirds like to sleep together all winter and make love for most of the spring whereupon the gentleman ladybird dies and the ladies are up and about needing to consume an enormous amount of any food they can find, especially aphids. After reproducing, the ladybirds are attracted back to their winter quarters by the scent of the dead gentleman's bodies. Someone who could synthesize the scent of dead gentleman ladybirds' bodies would make a fortune although there is probably some monk somewhere who is working on just that.

These aphids – on which the ladybird most likes to feed – can cause untold havoc and are usually blown in from France, Denmark or Belgium. Aphids are weak-engined and can't fly against the wind. Their taste buds are in their feet and their sex life is very complicated too even though they only make love once a year. After that the female aphids all become hard-line feminists having no need for men at all. They then breed like there's no tomorrow and if one aphid was left alone it would produce 600 million descendants a year.

But for the decisive intervention of the ladybird all our gardens and crops would be overwhelmed by seething beds of chomping aphids.

Not that Brother Anthony was slightly worried about any of that this hot, summer's day since, thanks to all his whirling ladybird visitors, not only were his beans doing fine but all his fruit was blooming, particularly the raspberries and blackcurrants. Clumps of reddening apples were hanging heavy on the branches. They were also having no trouble with water unlike others on the surrounding landscape since there were two deep wells in this monastery garden.

Elsewhere in the high new building of the monastery itself nothing seemed to come alive in the thick soupy air. All the monks were moving around slowly and thoughtfully like fish in an aquarium with almost every window open in the often forlorn hope of catching hold of a stray cooling breeze. This ferocious heat had been taking its toll on everyone and down in the grounds on a grassy bank underneath some oak and ash trees two men were covered with sweat as they dug a new grave in the rock hard clay.

It was quite cool last night, with some air around, but, as the dawn began to break, you could already sense the firm promise of yet more oxyacetylene hours that were about to attack everywhere and everyone regardless of their status. There was a new notice in the guest quarters asking everyone to draw the curtains in their bedrooms since all this sunshine could play havoc with the furniture. A lot of the monks quite simply stayed in their rooms. And sweated.

This early the main ambulatory of the monastery was empty except for the steady metronomic ticking of the grandfather clock. Dozens of rabbits were already out feeding on whatever they could find on the brown lawns, and from somewhere distant in the building echoed the sounds of a conversation. The rabbits emerged from their warrens which were directly underneath the monastery, grazing for a few moments before sitting upright, eyes alert and ears fully raised to pick up any sounds of impending danger.

Foxes regularly stroll past the rabbits but they are not perceived as dangerous and the rabbits barely look up at them. The monks believe that the foxes have long gone off stringy rabbit and prefer to eat something else. I'm with the foxes on this and have never anyway eaten a rabbit since reading *Watership Down*.

There was the ticking of the clock again broken now by a run of bells announcing the start of another important moment of the monastic day. Breakfast.

All meals are eaten in silence although breakfast is less formal than the other meals with a lot of coming and going. But I was already beginning to understand that each monastery has its own culture and habits even when they are of the same order. In Buckfast the dishes and cutlery were taken away to be washed in the kitchen but here the monks actually washed and cleaned their own dishes and cutlery with the aid of their fingers, napkins and bowls of water. One suggested that it was symbolic of the cleansing of the vessels at Mass but like the reasons for a lot of the other little rules that had evolved over the years no one was really certain.

But the one thing they certainly had in common was that they all bolted down their food without pause or hesitation, almost without tasting it, which could sometimes be thought to be a blessing particularly after a meal of Blood and Guts, about which more later. A public-school boy once told me that they always used to scoff down their food fast because they were afraid that someone else might pinch it. That was hardly likely to happen here in a Benedictine monastery although one monk told me that they did eat quickly because they were not supposed to hold up any of the others. Another said the sooner they finished the sooner they could get to their free periods. Benedictines always take a pride, I've long noticed, in being unsentimental and clear-headed. If those rabbits under the monastery began undermining the foundations, well, they would just gas them.

Already the first of the day's many wasps were up and around the breakfast table, sniffing around the marmalade or seeking any other sugary delights. Some of the monks simply ignored the wasps but others swatted them away with the backs of their hands. When they had finished washing their own dishes and cutlery they each took a small wooden pan and brush to clean up the polished table around them. Any stray bits of food that were left were often picked up on the tips of their fingers and popped into their mouths.

Birds were now dropping down among the rabbits on the brown lawns outside but they weren't having too much luck either since the growing heat had already driven the worms deep in their search for moisture. The stricken shrieks of peacocks came from the nearby bird park where many of the birds had already begun moulting. A lot of the monks had done their private offices in the cool of the early morning in their rooms but there was still a whole, hot day to get through.

The practice of prayer is fundamental to life at Prinknash and in Matins I again studied each and every of the twenty or so monks' faces closely. When I pray my mind wanders all over the shop and, if lucky, I can manage to focus a slight beam of illuminating light on something deep in the darkness. But these monks seemed to be right there in the light of the darkness and, despite the heat, I never did once notice an apparent lapse of concentration or any other signs of a wandering mind or going through the motions.

The reason we exist is to seek God, Father Stephen told me. We can only find him through prayer.

By now the sun had climbed ever higher in the blue sky with the monks dispersing to start on their day jobs and there was much to do in this large monastery ranging from work on the lawn and garden to that on stained glass and iron. The pottery has been the largest of these industries since the monks found the clay on the estate which was perfect for ceramic work. They then sold it throughout the world, using the money to help build themselves a new abbey here in the Vale of Gloucestershire, about half a mile away from the old one, the magnificent St Peter's Grange on the other side of the valley and now used as a retreat house.

They also blend incense from resinous gum and perfumes and, apart from being guest master, Father Stephen helps out in there. But he does find this work difficult in this heat particularly as it can aggravate his asthma.

There was one monk, however, who actually thrived on this heat and enjoyed it. This was Brother Bartholomew – known to many as Bart – who reckoned it was all cool by his normal standards since he was here for the summer from Ghana in Africa and his skin was as black as night. He didn't even mind wielding the pick as they attacked that grave again, loosening up his rippling black shoulders and whacking it down with gusto. They had been digging the grave for most of the morning, chipping down through inch after unyielding inch into a clay bed which was known to be at least 125ft deep.

Fat carp were rising to the surface in the medieval fish ponds in the bird park searching for any relieving oxygen as the first visitors of the day stepped off the buses in the car parks and sat around on the picnic benches in the shade fanning themselves.

One of the bus drivers was lying on his driving seat with his stockinged feet sticking out of the window and enjoying a cigarette and down near the pottery a dog was stretched out under a tree looking extremely fed up. He had clearly been rolling around in the grass a lot judging by the bits all over him, almost certainly trying to do something about the fleas which, brought alive by the heat, had taken up lodgings in his coat.

The new monastery here was only consecrated in 1972 and the bells were still on a temporary structure in the garden, quietly awaiting their own belfry. But St Peter's Grange, the old monastery and original settlement here, seemed far cooler and more suited to this type of weather. Indeed it was almost an oasis of stone, dark wood and antique furniture where you could actually breathe without it seeming that you were trying to swallow balls of cotton wool. Just being inside the fine medieval chapel you would be hard pushed to think that you were in a heat wave at all. Just sitting there was like quietly sucking on an ice-lolly.

The monk in charge believed that the stone building absorbed a lot of moisture in the cold of winter which was then released in the heat of the summer setting up a form of refrigeration. Certainly it was a marvellous release from the heat to sit in the choir stalls of the chapel, admiring the frothing stonework of the master craftsmen around the rear of the altar and reflecting on how those Benedictine monks must have first come here in 1928 after finding life on Caldey Island off the coast of Pembrokeshire too difficult and selling it to the Cistercians.

It was a wild and ragged island was this Caldey; a place set apart when I was there two years ago, accessible only by boat across the treacherous seas of Caldey Sound and out of the port of Tenby.

Many of the islanders were on the jetty when we pulled in, going off to Tenby for a day of shopping, and I duly wandered up the ragged stone path, soon finding that I all but had the island to myself since I had arrived, uninvited and unannounced, out of the tourist season. The shops were closed and the monastery doors locked. Almost immediately I picked up some of the chilliness of the island which may have driven the Benedictines away all those years earlier.

I struck out along the high headlands feeling a tremendous sense of isolation, looking down at the black kelp rising up and down in the white heads of the waves which kept beating against the red sandstone cliffs. In one hidden grove there was a ramshackle wooden hermitage overlooking the sea, with a tiny windmill on its roof to generate electricity. PRIVATE, it said on a notice. There were lots of other signs which said KEEP OUT and NO ENTRY and PRIVATE BEACH. There was also lots of barbed wire along the public paths, all of it reinforcing my growing sense of isolation.

I walked into a farmyard and approached a burly, bearded farmer who said that he wasn't interested in talking to me but I should try his wife who was clipping ivy at the side of the stable. But it turned out that she was even less interested in talking to me than her husband, complaining that lies were always being written about the island.

Deep in another wood there was a sparkly grotto built to the Virgin Mary and, way along that cliff, an unattended light-house. Manx shearwaters skimmed the waves and, down in the deep throats of the coves, there were lolling seals. They say that every flower mentioned by Shakespeare grows on Caldey but, even crowned in warm sunshine as it was that day, I never once felt at ease in this beflowered place, finding it cold and unwelcoming.

The monastery itself sat, majestic and aloof, in a dip between some wooded hills with white towers and a red-tiled roof. The Cistercians there follow a vow of silence and I couldn't find anyone prepared to talk to a pilgrim at the gate. Neither had I been offered any food so I sat alone for many hours in the deserted village occasionally wandering off to eat some black-berries as I waited, with no little impatience, for the boat to take me back to Tenby. You can't, as they say, win them all.

Down in the monks' small cemetery in Prinknash two monks and Donald Borzoni, a retreatant, had again become as moles, attacking the unyielding clay with a pick and shovel, the dirt flying up into the air out of their growing hole in fitful fountains, now hitting on a huge boulder with no real idea of how big it was. But it would have to come out since Brother Giles, the monk in charge of digging graves absolutely insisted on straight walls and a perfect shape for all his graves.

This perfectly shaped grave was for Father Oswald who had died a few days earlier, aged 92, I had learned. He was a fine, much-loved monk who had got infirm and a bit dithery in his later years and there had been a lot of prayer for his final release. 'Where am I?' he would ask. 'In a monastery.' 'Why am I here?' 'Because you're a monk.' 'How did I become a monk then?'

The other monks had looked after him with a faithful and careful diligence and Father Oswald even occasionally showed that he was still a fine piano player until last Monday when the heat seemed to be really getting to him. He had stood up from his normal place in the refectory and walked out but then, for some reason, walked back again and sat down on his chair only to fall over and hit his head, possibly on the leg of the table. The other monks got him to his room with a large bump on his head and he seemed to be all right except that he began haemorrhaging in the middle of the night, when a doctor was called and he died. The funeral was due to take place the following Friday.

That night I went back to the monks' graves and sat with them on my own in the thickening twilight. The cemetery was merely a row of simple wooden crosses most pleasing, you could be sure, to the son of a carpenter who delighted in everything that was simple, lowly and humble. Distant sounds of traffic carried in the hot, still darkness and bats came out with their teeth snatching insects out of the air.

I kept catching myself ducking as they swooped low over my head but then remembered that bats were lovely creatures; yet more radiant jewels in the rich and textured crown of God's creation. They are warm-blooded and extremely sociable, I had learned. The mother has one baby a year and looks after it in a sort of nursery with all the others. They are also extremely clean and even beautiful if you look at their faces from a certain angle. If you do ever come face to face with one then note the long ears with the second set of ears inside them. Mark the squinty eyes and the upturned bulldog snout. They also have a thick growth of hair along their foreheads rather like a guardsman's busby.

I was once taken to a derelict mansion here in the Cotswolds to look at a swarm of roosting bats and, together with the births of my children, it remains one of the great moments of my life. The house looked like a fragment of a lovely dissolving dream as we approached it in the dying light of the day and once inside we came across some blackbirds squabbling noisily in the ruined chapel. Saplings grew in the mildewed corridors and, all over the steps of the great stone stairs, were scatterings of rubble. We climbed high to the top floor and into a carpeted hide where, with the aid of an image and light intensifier, I was able to gaze at a colony of greater horseshoe bats all hanging together and preening themselves.

It was so moving – a moment given for ever – just lying there and listening to their quiet flutterings, amplified slightly by the emptiness of the roof space. There might have been thirty of them hanging there together in a huge, furry pendant, their heads and eyes sticking out in every direction and, for all I knew, it could have been one of those same bats which was now hunting for insects above the empty grave which, with an open-mouthed and resolute patience, was now awaiting delivery of the body of dear Father Oswald.

Yes, this time of bats above an empty grave was clearly yet another of my pilgrim moments although, in a privileged life of a journalist and writer, there have probably been many such moments when, being close to all the symbols of death and destruction, my mind has been able to reach out and seize on a fantastic memory of life. Somewhere you should always be able to find a vein of love and beauty running through even your worst moments and when you can keep finding this vein, despite all the odds, perhaps you can then call yourself a true pilgrim: one who shuns the violent, the cruel and the ugly and who is merely called to be a witness to the transcendent innocence and beauty of an ordinary world.

Father Oswald's body was laid to rest in the chapel the next day with the full service of The Receiving of the Body. The monks then continued conducting their rites of love around the coffin which just lay there in perfect peace and repose.

On top of the coffin, which had small wooden handles, they had lain Oswald's Greek Breviary, his silver chalice and stole and a simple rosary given to him by Father Fabian.

At Compline that night God seemed to have moved closer to everyone in the grieving, praying darkness and you sensed that the death of their beloved Oswald had brought these monks of Prinknash closer to the deep meanings and truths for which they all clearly craved and had given everything up to find. The Gregorian chants were exquisite; the melancholy voices unusually beautiful. The life of the monastery had entered into the death of Oswald and made itself deeper and richer and wholer in the process. Just like the sacrifice of their Master on the cross, Oswald's death had given them more life. Another flame had been passed on that they could live more abundantly.

My sleep that night was deep and fresh, untroubled by dreams of roaring, ferocious lions or even fluttering, friendly bats.

The next morning Father Oswald was buried with the full Requiem Mass. There were about fifty present which included twenty or so monks, the estate workers, a visiting abbot and about six oblates: lay people associated with the order in prayer. The only members of Oswald's family were a nephew and his wife who, you could tell by the uncertainty of their movements, knew little of the rituals of Catholic worship.

Oswald had been a pharmacist by profession, we learned in the eulogy by Father Francis, and had taught himself Latin and Greek. He had been working on a translation from Greek of the letters of one of the saints before he had fallen ill. He was also an absolutely lousy cook, Father Francis added to a roar of laughter, who once, with another academic, the late Father Sylvester, served up beetroot juice and macaroni, dreadful to look at and even worse to taste, and known thereafter as Blood and Guts.

The coffin sat quietly throughout the prayer and laughter looking as if it was already being burnished by the hands of busy angels in the coloured streams of the light of the sun striking the stained-glass windows. At the end of the Mass Oswald was taken out of the chapel feet first when, for some reason I never did quite discover, we more ordinary mortals are always taken out head first.

The coffin was then lowered into the waiting grave beneath the oak and ash trees surrounded by the monks and sprinkled with holy water. Father Francis shook hands with the two relatives who paid their last respects and left. Later, after lunch, Donald Borzoni and Brother Giles really got down to it with their shovels, filling in the grave which had taken so long to dig in a straight two hours without a break or pause.

But by the time they had finished their labours the monastery had long settled back into its quiet and unbending rhythms in this long sweltering summer without end. And the angels had long carried up Father Oswald in their arms over the Jordan to receive his just and fitting reward.

FIVE

A Stairway to Heaven

IT HAD BEGUN spattering with a light rain for the first time for weeks when I wandered around St Martin's churchyard in North Nibley and began my search for another English hero who had once so wonderfully raised the roof and shaken the rafters.

William Tyndale was his name and I had been knocking on doors in the neighbourhood asking about this Gloucestershire son who had defied Rome back in the early sixteenth century, not only translating the Bible from the original Greek into 'the tongue of the people' but also denying such key Catholic doctrines as transubstantiation for which he was later ritually strangled and burned at the stake in Belgium. The Church at the time never did see much point in discussion or argument.

There has always been something about these Lutheran rebel dogs that have greatly appealed to me so I had hoped to pick up something about Tyndale's life and personality by digging around in the haunts of his youth about which, it has to be said immediately, little is known with any certainty.

No one is even sure where Tyndale was born although tradition has it that he was christened here in St Martin's, and so I entered that graveyard carefully and watchfully first noting a big black cat sitting on top of one of the ivy-throttled tombstones where he was was peering down into the high undergrowth clearly interested in something small and furry which he was about to pounce on and eat. By the side of the main door was an old and rusty plough reminding you that it was for the workers of the land that Tyndale had made his translation.

The spots of rain hit the dry earth and seemed to just disappear into it. The long cracks and fissures still ran every which way needing to be filled with a lot more rain yet before they were going to close up.

This was one of those churchyards which were a part of the Living Churchyard scheme, I learned from a plaque in the vestry and, inside, children had pinned up their projects on what they

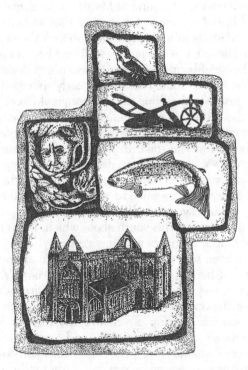

had found in this churchyard. They had found fungi, woodlice, fleas and spiders. They had also found owl pellets, snail shells and caterpillars. One was clearly pleased to have found one big hole.

Churches like this, we have often been told, are their own Bibles in stone, wood and glass, telling us much about the history and beliefs of the area. A list of incumbents over the south aisle doorway told of a ministry here late in the twelfth century. On one of the octagonal pillars is a carving of the Green Man so often found in medieval country churches with his flowing moustache changing into tendrils and leafy branches. A symbol of the Foresters, the Green Man was also thought to have inspired the myths of the outlaw Robin Hood. This graveyard also, it is believed, contains the graves of those killed in the last private battle between barons in England.

But the building itself is not unique in any way and its roof looks as if it is going to fly away or fall down at any minute. Indeed it is a haphazard blend of fifteenth, seventeenth and nineteenth-century architecture but it does perhaps mirror the simple rural community of the Severn Vale which once, as simple communities can sometimes do, threw up a man who, with the thunder and lightning of his personality, changed the world. Not that there was anything simple or too rural about the Tyndale family, I was later to learn, since they were clearly seriously rich.

And neither had Tyndale been forgotten to this day since elsewhere in North Nibley there was a Tyndale Close, a Tyndale Old People's Home and a new plaque on the side of the primary school commemorating the quincentenary of his birth. One huge monument to him towers over the whole village and the Severn Valley in the shape of the high, pencil-sharp stone tower on Nibley Knoll erected in 1886.

It kept raining fitfully when I followed the path up the Knoll through a dense overhanging wood where the light kept shifting about in the drizzle. I sat outside the base of the monument under the shelter of my golf umbrella, sucking on a mint as I thought of that man who once pledged that, thanks to his efforts, the boy who drives the plough shall know more of the Scriptures than the clergy. Tyndale used the language of the farm worker in his mighty work too, giving us such sayings as 'the salt of the earth', 'the signs of the times' and 'the powers that be'. The language of his translation was the language of the Severn Vale, it was said.

He was very much a man of his time, under the influence of the Reformation and given to the most violent attacks on the Establishment. His greatest attacks were on Thomas Moore and the Pope, never pulling back or mincing his words. When he hit out he always hit hard. Only two of his Bibles survived, one bought by the British Museum and another in a Baptist College in Bristol. But it was not for his translations that he was burned at the stake so much as for his constant and virulent attacks on the Pope.

There had been much consternation in the village recently since the local youngsters had thrown a series of two-day rave parties in the field around this monument. Quite what Tyndale would have made of all those flashing lights and dance music is anyone's guess but we know for certain that the local worthies absolutely hated it. They complained bitterly to the parish council and got posts erected at the entrance to the path up this Knoll to stop any of the ravers getting up there in their cars with their 'infernal' amplification equipment merely to dance about to their 'jungle' music. We are not having anyone around here actually enjoying themselves, by jove. I mean who do they think they are?

The house most commonly connected with the Tyndale family is Hunts Court on the other side of the village which was once a farm but is now a garden nursery owned by Keith Marshall. We don't know if Tyndale was born there but it was certainly once owned by the Tyndale family, who must have been very wealthy for the times, and last year they staged a play about the life of Tyndale in the courtyard. Keith Marshall showed me around his amazing old house which has been patched here and there with modern bits. 'There's not a wall that's straight, a corner that's square or a floor that's flat but what the hell?' He added that he could hear the death-watch beetle tapping away in the rafters every spring but wouldn't have it any other way.

The other home which has long been associated with the Tyndale family is Melcham Court in the next parish of Stinchcombe and this really is an astonishing wisteria-clad pile of

Cotswold stone and mullioned window sitting in huge formal gardens and looking rather like something that an oil billionaire and a royal architect might have cooked up on the telephone.

This lump of paradise had recently been bought by Roger Maggs, a Welshman from Ammanford, who showed me around his gardens with a swimming pool and an arboretum, a waterfall and a stone barn with a minstrel gallery. The garden was so large he needed four gardeners to keep it under control, while the house itself was a quiet symphony of old wood and stone. The builders had recently discovered a deep well in the back kitchen which he was not too sure what to do with. It would be quite useful for drowning yourself in, I thought but, apart from that, it didn't have any other clear use and there were some thoughts of filling it in.

As soon as he drove up around the corner of the drive and saw Melcham Court he was smitten, he said, making immediate plans to retire from his job in Canada. I knew exactly how he felt. Every inch of the place was beautiful. There are only two or three houses in the country that have ever made me feel irrationally sick with envy and that was one of them.

Thinking about the house again afterwards – as I did frequently in the way one might also think of an extravagantly beautiful woman one had just met – I thought of Laurie Lee's seventeenth-century Cotswold cottage with 'hand-carved windows, golden surfaces, moss-flaked tiles and walls so thick they kept a damp chill inside them whatever the season'. It always smelt of pepper and mushrooms, Laurie said. The moss on the tiles sparkled like crystallized honey.

Laurie wrote like an angel but he was a very strange man, I remembered, seeing again his craggy face which made him look like a professional boxer who had seen the business end of too many punches. Once while I was sitting with him at a 'freebie' lunch for something or other in The Savoy he was given a glass of green chartreuse. He decided after much loud debate with himself that he didn't want to drink it right there but, rather than leave it, he took a brown envelope out of his inside pocket in which nestled a gas bill. He duly poured the green chartreuse into this envelope and put it back into his pocket with an ensuing mess all over his suit which is probably all too easy to imagine.

The other former haunt of the youthful Tyndale and his family was the nearby village of Slimbridge and here again I found myself slipping and struggling in one of my strange pilgrim dreams. But they weren't of ferocious lions this time since I was standing in a clearing of trembling light surrounded by dozens of pink flamingos with their bent black beaks, question-mark necks and most of them standing around in the water on one leg like some exotic gang which had just been discharged from a particularly efficient clinic for amputating limbs.

All around were other lagoons edged by willow and ash trees, again gathering up all this trembling light as ducks wandered towards me to peck at my trouser legs while the thick humid air was alive with banshee jabber and strange chuckling. I could have been in a hot, tropical jungle in darkest Africa as another gang of geese began mumbling on flat harmonicas as they harassed me for food.

Yet it was the horrible – and I mean the nose-bleedingly horrible – smell of the flamingos which told me that this was not another of my pilgrim dreams since I was in fact wandering through the wonderful Wildfowl Trust in Slimbridge, founded by the late Peter Scott, proof positive that where one great Englishman had once walked and lived then so too had another. Both Tyndale and Scott were the two sides of the same coin; defiant and courageous, fighting everything and anyone to realize their deepest ambitions and dreams.

Later that afternoon the sunshine was still mingling with the rain as I stood on the edge of the Severn Estuary looking out at the new Severn Bridge just nearing completion. The curving, sun-kissed wires and lines of the bridge seemed to be floating on the mists and it struck me then that this was exactly what a stairway to heaven might look like, particularly as the bridge was, in fact, leading to that great and fabled kingdom of Wales.

Rivers have a wider range of moods than an Italian opera diva. Sometimes they will trickle around and dawdle like that small boy making his unwilling way to school and at others they will roar and spill forwards as if driven by some internal tempest. Today the pool-and-riffle curves of the River Wye, stirred up by nearly a week of intermittent rains, were running determinedly like a man head down through rush hour crowds, impatient to get back to the warm and soothing sanctuary of his home after a frenzied day at the office. He was thinking of slippers and tea and a fire and was completely obsessed by this vision, hardly taking any notice of anyone around him or anything on either of his banks as he strode on down past old mills and beneath even older iron bridges, turning right to round a wooded escarpment then turning a sharp left to round another, as he rushed from pool to pool . . . shoaling, riffling, deepening . . . in the way that rivers – and impatient home-going office workers – do.

It had probably sprung with much the same impatience out of the very bowels of the land in Plynlimon on the Cambrian Mountains, oozing up out of the very pores of the land before bowling down through Herefordshire, determined to keep that most urgent of appointments with the great tidal rips of the Severn Estuary. A group of youngsters in multi-coloured anoraks cycled past on the other bank and a woodsman was cutting wood and burning it with a fire which glowed with a fierce, red heart. The cyclists let loose a burst of foul language which hung discordantly like the smell of a piggery in this pure valley air.

Occasionally you can spot a salmon making a huge, triumphant leap as it vaults up out of the hurrying torrents, bending almost double in an arc of flashy exuberance before falling back into the water. Lying flat on a boulder and gazing deep down into a quiet pool I could see all kinds of other darting mazey movements which I could not identify since no fewer than twenty-nine other species of fish hang around in this river, from tiny sticklebacks to rainbow trout and millions of wriggling eels.

William Wordsworth detected 'a soft inland murmur' in this river but, lying flat on that boulder, I couldn't help but marvel that something so big and so eager and so smoothly fast made so little noise. It was completely silent and, closing my eyes, I could hear the cry of a sheep, a passing car, a skylark, a magpie, a breeze lifting the leaves of an overhanging tree into a round of applause . . . but nothing, not even a soft inland murmur, coming from the river itself.

A thick swarm of mullet were feeding in the weeds with their bellies turning from white to silver as they caught the light. Further down, a fisherman was standing up to this waist in the river as he cast and recast his line. Those mullet just won't take his bait, he said. They seem to know what's going on and would just stand looking at his bait all day if necessary, he added. Further on again a few mallard ducks were mooching about on their own.

I had stopped in Redbrook, chatting to a man with an old antique shop there, who told me that the salmon and fishermen had only recently reappeared after going missing for around six weeks in the drought. But, now the rains had filled up the river again, the salmon had come back, fighting their way home again, just as they have since time immemorial. There had never been any industry on the Wye and hence no pollution. There were otters, heron and kingfishers around here too, he said, reminding you that the river is the basic artery of the land and that water, as the bringer and giver of all life, is the prime material of God, the means of baptism, faith and regeneration. From water we come and to water we will return.

I carried on down along the river bank coming to the Old Railway Station at Tintern, once the end of a small rural line and now a pleasant picnic area with grass lawns where the trains used to run. There are the old broken-necked red and white signals, a craft shop in the signal box and a small restaurant in the old waiting rooms where you will now need 55p for a cup of tea or 60p for a mug. They've kept a lot of the old signs here too, including that old favourite now sadly deceased: *Gentlemen, please adjust your dress before leaving*.

A cup of tea and a ham sandwich later I walked on down into Tintern following the great, silent river again until it took me past an old mill and out in front of the gut-wrenching ruins of the abbey, still managing to look like the great if ageing actress she was, just sitting there in this amazing woodland valley, and making your knees go quite wobbly as you tottered towards her wondering if she was really holding out her arms to welcome lucky old you.

The abbey ruin has colonized the delta-like flatland with a serene and even disdainful arrogance and just being near her you somehow understood why all those painters and poets had been attracted to these 'bare, ruined choirs where late the sweet birds sang'. Wordsworth composed a famous poem to this ruin; J. M. W. Turner immortalized it in one of his great paintings although one writer, a William Gilpin, didn't think that the ruins were quite ruined enough, claiming that some of the gable ends were, in fact, rather vulgar and arguing, perhaps with tongue in cheek, that someone should get a mallet and try rearranging them a bit. Even in 1800 this place was a busy tourist attraction with boat-loads of tourists brought up from Chepstow.

But the modern pilgrim can today hire a new device in the ticket office which will propel him straight back into the beginnings of the abbey since they now have the Walkman guide which will take you around the ruins while also recreating the sounds, chanting and prayer of old. The transport is complete as you are moved back one century after another until you are right there again, with the cowl of your robe pulled well down over your head to protect you from the ferocious cold of winter.

Certainly I felt as one with the building almost as soon as I put on my earphones and my sandalled feet were walking towards the cloisters to catch Collation, an unusual event in any Cistercian monastery so far as I know since this was a reading from the Scriptures which took place in the cloisters before Compline. The abbot always liked us to be on time for this one and there'd been some fuss lately because the choir monks were getting later and later in leaving their studies. Collation is as important as Compline the abbot had kept going on. *I want you all there*.

The bells rang again and you could almost hear the abbot's exasperation in them since many of the monks still had their tonsured heads buried in their books. We weren't responding to him as we might any longer, I thought, largely because it was getting so bitterly cold this long, hard winter and the food was getting so poor. Many of us were even becoming a bad-tempered Athenian rabble, forever rushing to the warming house where we jigged around in front of the fire and massaged our limbs until the prior came along and shooed us out. The food kept getting worse and worse as well unless you liked bread and cheese. Meat was only allowed for those convalescing from an illness in the infirmary and there was a fair bit of dishonest competition to get your head down on a pillow in there.

With this collapse in our discipline came a corresponding collapse in our prayer life. The whole abbey seemed to lose her tenacity and vigour with a few going out drinking and wooing impressionable young farm girls. Public support drifted away too until 1536 when there were were but twelve choir monks left here with some 35 monastic servants. Some three servants for every monk! Dissolution became almost inevitable – there was no one prepared to fight our corner after all – with the abbey treasures all sent to the king's treasury and the lead stripped off the roof. The abbey soon fell into chronic decay.

Historians usually blame King Henry VIII for this sorry state of affairs but I'm here to tell you the real truth which was that we had all turned our back on God and, when we did that, God gave us up. It was all as simple as that.

Today all the cloisters have been broken up with bird droppings and white matted feathers everywhere. The only tomb lies under the north arch: *Hic: Iacet: Nicholas: Landaverists* – Here lies Nicholas of Llandaff. Stone bosses lay around the neatly manicured lawns. There was once coloured glass in the great west window which transformed the nave into a heavenly vision in the sunlight. But now the empty window frames views of river and wood with a red hot-air balloon floating peacefully over the valley.

At Compline we pulled our hoods down even further to keep out the cold and reinforce our deep desire for oneness with God. Prayers were chanted around the guttering candles as the abbot sprinkled holy water over us in a final act of purification.

The water drops hit against my face with a sharp and almost needle-like coldness and I opened my eyes to look up at the gaping space where there had once been a roof. The skies were curdling black again and, looking out over the huge, silent river as it continued winding its way down the valley, I knew that our long, hot summer was over and that we were now in for weeks and weeks of hard rain.

SIX
Greenbelt Ghosts

IT WAS A grey, warm Sunday morning and hundreds were
milling across the fields and down the slopes to gather in
a huge grassy bowl in front of a stage. Some were carrying flags and others had painted faces and plaited hair. Yet
more were pitching up and there was the faint impression
of massing warriors getting together for some strange tribal
dance. Singers were gathering on the stage and practising. *La –
la – la – laah. La – la – la – laah.* Six huge crosses appeared but
they were not of the simple, wooden type since they had been
made from beer tins, Coca-Cola cans and barbed wire. *La – la –
la – lah.*

These massing tribes, you soon noticed, seemed to have
a deep terror of appearing dull or drab. Understatement
was nowhere in evidence. Everything from their hats to their
vests and right down to their bootlaces were of the brightest and gaudiest hue. There was a lot of raucous laughter too
and a few of the young girls were puffing on cigarettes. Those
singers were still practising their scales and there was one
of those agonizing screeches of static as a guitar was plugged
into an amplifier and tuned. *La – la – la – laah. La – la –
la – laah.*

Everywhere the slopes were dotted with bits of dried cow
dung which had to be kicked away carefully before they sat
down. Swallows were out hunting for food, swooping down low
over the heads of the gathering crowds. We had come to Deene
Park, deep in the wilds of Northamptonshire.

Some music began playing softly with a flute weaving its
sorrowful way through it. Now the flute began trilling and a girl's
voice sang: 'Come Holy Spirit'. There was a massed response of
'Come Holy Spirit. Maranatha. Come Lord, come.'

Breath of God.
Breath of life.
Breath for Tomorrow.

MARANATHA

Comforter.
　　Disturber.
　　　　Heavenly Friend.
　　　　　　Revealer of Truth.

Good morning and a warm welcome to our communion service at Greenbelt '95. The theme of this service reflects the theme of this year's festival – dry bones dancing – and is inspired by Ezekiel's vision in the valley of dry bones.

> The hand of the Lord was upon me, and he brought me out by the Spirit of the Lord and set me in the middle of a valley; it was full of bones. He led me to and fro among them and I saw a great many bones on the floor of the valley, bones that were very dry. He asked me: 'Son of Man can these bones live?' I said: 'Oh Sovereign Lord you alone know.' Then he said to me: 'Prophesy to these bones and say unto them. "Dry bones hear the word of the Lord. This is what the Sovereign Lord says to these bones: I will make breath enter you so you will come to life."'

It had been just after four in the morning and, unable to sleep in my camper van the night before, I had been walking around the festival site on my own. The roof of the sky was studded with stars and occasionally a blustery wind shook the canvas walls of the sleeping tents like ghosts demanding to be let inside.

The main sound was the humming of the massive generators but, otherwise, it was a few hours of welcome silence as a couple of security guards with their walkie-talkies wandered along the fences, through the orange sodium glow of the lights and past the marooned marquees, all tethered and quiet now, awaiting the gabbling, swarming bedlam to come.

On the outlying slopes were thousands of smaller tents and, again, little could be heard out there either except the odd pull of a tent zip when a stooped figure might hurry towards a hedge to urinate, doubtless hoping that no one could see him in the darkness. Right in front of the main entrance was a gnarled and dead tree and, over the way again, were lines of food stalls which would soon be selling everything from crepes to spare ribs and baked potatoes or Japanese noodles to the hungry multitudes who, just for the moment, were only concerned with snoozing in their sleeping bags.

Each of the main marquees were named after deserts – Gobi, Sahara, Nevada, Kalahari – and, just lingering awhile inside their emptiness with that peculiar smell of airlessness and crushed grass that you find inside all marquees, I heard again the voices and words of all the hundreds of seminars that I have heard in these tents over the years. Here there have been men and women who seem not to have been assailed by a second of doubt as they grabbed the lectern and answered such big questions as: Is football a bigger religion than Christianity? Is *Pulp Fiction* biblical? Has God saved the Queen? Or why, if he could topple tyrants, did Jesus end up getting himself executed by a provincial governor?

The problem is to split the police from his uniform and find the humanity of that person . . .

There is simply no way that God can forgive Geoffrey Dahmer . . .

If Jesus meant the Sermon on the Mount then why are there so few castrated, one-eyed, one-armed Christians around? Well, I'm now going to tell you why . . .

And I am here to tell you, with all the moral authority that I believe that God has invested in me, that if you could somehow get television out of Northern Ireland then that civil conflict would be over for good . . .

I smiled as I heard all those voices again, all of them spinning out of the crushed grass airlessness; all of them rising up in jokes and fury, in ecstasy and pain; all of them with their own exclusive handles on the meanings of the wild word of God and what he was this very minute so desperately trying to tell his collapsing kingdom. *I want you to prophesy to all those dry bones.*

Walking on into the night again I remembered all the great characters I've met over the years I've been coming to Greenbelt, from the black girl who was hoping to write a novel in five minutes to the Australian who had set up a ministry with the Hell's Angels, and Griff, the musician with no tunes and unintelligible words who always attracted hundreds whenever he opened his mouth and sang his truly appalling songs.

Then there was Stewart Henderson, the Christian poet with whom I whiled away some of my happiest ever hours chatting as we walked around Jerusalem, and Steve Fairnie, that strange Bristolian who looked like a cross between Adolf Hitler and Charlie Chaplin. He had a great singing act with his ravishing wife Bev but his speciality was hypnotizing chickens, once putting five of them out – and a dog who happened to be watching the act – all of them flat on their backs with their legs poking straight up into the air.

Steve died unexpectedly a few years back but his spirit continues to live with us all as closely as the secret dust in the linings of our pockets. He was there by my side still, a part of all of us at Greenbelt for all time, as I stood watching the dawn break and hundreds of heads came poking out of their tents, all now scuffling their hair with their hands and peering around blearily as they appeared to troop down for the communion service this grey, warm Sunday morning.

Son of Man can these dry bones live? I am Gustavo Parajon from Nicaragua. I bring you greetings from the Protestant Council of Churches and from my own, the First Baptist Church in Managua.

Nicaragua was of great interest to the news in the 80s when people saw what was happening there as a sign of hope for the oppressed. In 1990 there was a dramatic change in our lives and we began to experience the impact of the policies of the World Bank and the International Monetary Fund on us. A great number of us – some 60 per cent – had no jobs. Poverty had reached 74 per cent of our population. The poor did not have access to medical care. The doors for our children to be educated at primary, secondary and university level are closed. In Nicaragua there is disillusion with politics and politicians; a great sadness for the sacrifice of the 80s and the loss of so many lives. There seems no hope for the future. The most powerful and wealthy countries control our lives.

This passage from Ezekiel could very well apply to us. It would appear that the bones are very dry in the valley of Nicaragua. But what a challenge to Ezekiel. God did not need to invite Ezekiel to prophesy but he was inviting us to prophesy to the world and dry bones. If we read the one chapter we see how the stream shall become a powerful river. This stream comes from the altar. This stream turns everything in the valley into life.

God does this through the Holy Spirit. But God also asked Ezekiel to participate and prophesy. God challenges Ezekiel: Can these dry bones live? Ezekiel was as doubtful as we are in Nicaragua when we do not see an end to suffering. Ezekiel says: Only you Lord know. So the order comes: Prophesy and I will breathe the spirit into these dry bones. It is that conviction that God is in charge of history that gives us a lot of hope. When Abraham saw his body as good as dead and his wife Sarah barren, yet he believed and God made his promise good.

We have all felt the breath of God and the spirit among us. Despite our agony we can see our villages with their women and children in the presence of the Lord promising life. We see the women saving pennies to buy nets to go out and fish for their children. These faithful women have pooled their resources and made a tremendous difference.

When you help us you are living witnesses; you are leading us to the power of the Spirit which led Ezekiel to say: Breathe, Oh Spirit of God. This Spirit has changed our lives and shows that God is challenging his church to prophesy. The Spirit is challenging us that even though we may be dry bones we can become the channel and waters of life. Amen.

Yesterday afternoon the huge oak trees looking down on the giant Meccano stage caught a blast of rock 'n' roll and sighed.

Music is at the very centre of the Greenbelt experience and right at that moment there were five bands all pounding away furiously as if their mothers were going to confiscate all their instruments at any second. One band was trying to take the roof off the main stage and the others in their marquees, with the distinctive thump of the bass and crack of drums, all made it sound as if half a dozen Red Indian war parties were busy working themselves up for a good bout of fighting and scalping.

There have been some truly great acts here over the years and there have been some truly dreadful ones too, over which it is probably best to draw a discreet veil. But good or bad they are all usually seeking to renew and extend the kingdom with their music as well as enjoying one another's fellowship. 'I always come to this weekend and love discussing new ideas with the others,' said the truly awesome singer Martyn Joseph. 'When I leave I always feel I've been touched by something.'

My personal favourite has always been the hot, driving rhythms of the gospel choirs and until you have woken up and eaten a breakfast of a bacon and egg roll sitting at the feet of the London Gospel Choir as their fantastic Pentecostal joy took everything higher and wilder – and you got egg dribbling all over your chin and the front of your shirt but didn't give a damn – then you have never really woken up and had breakfast.

The Fringe, on the other hand, attracts musicians who can play and musicians who clearly can't; musicians who would like to play and others who would never hit the right notes even after thousands of years of practice. Many share the faith but a lot don't, but they are all welcome with the quiet prayer that something of the joy of the kingdom will rub off on them.

This weekend we will be listening to the special Bruce Cockburn and the dazzling Celtic riffs of the band Iona.

We have heard from Gustavo about the dry bones in his community. Now I want you all to break up into groups and quietly reflect on the pain and brokenness we see here in our own communities.

When we have struck down others with our callous words and deeds, casting stones on their dreams and hopes until they are broken . . . then break us, O Lord.

When we have persecuted others, labelling them, judging them, cursing them, leaving them forsaken . . . then break us, O Lord.

When we have abandoned others in our comfortable lives and in our silent support of systems which oppress . . . then break us, O Lord.

By the power of the Holy Spirit who repairs our brokenness, breathing life into dry bones as on the day of resurrection, renew and resurrect us for Jesus' sake. Amen.

So I prophesied as I was commanded. And as I was prophesying there was a noise, a rattling sound and the bones came together, bone to bone. I looked and tendons and flesh appeared on them and skin covered them, but there was no breath in them.

Then he said to me: 'Prophesy to the breath; prophesy, son of man, and say to it, "This is what the Sovereign Lord says: Come from the four winds, O breath, and breathe into these slain that they may live."' So I prophesied as he commanded me, and breath entered them; they came to life and stood up on their feet – a vast army.

My name is Frank Chikane. I am from South Africa and am based in Cape Town. I bring greetings to you all from the churches and people in South Africa. I also want to thank you for your support throughout the world for the miracle that's happening there. We should give ourselves a big hand and God an even bigger one for the miracle in South Africa.

The story of the dry bones and the spirit which gives life to dry bones is symbolic of our experience in South Africa. We have come out of a darkness where there was no hope at all. We were at the end.

We were known as the country with the worst form of institutionalized racism ever experienced. It was declared a crime against humanity by the United Nations. I come from a country which had the worst form of oppression against her people.

I come from a country with a most sophisticated military machine with a nuclear capability and chemical weapons ready to be used against us.

I come from a country where if you looked at reality you would have said that there was no hope at all because there was nothing you could do about it. It looked hopeless.

The gallant support we got from the world can only be described as an act of faith. In terms of reality it did not make sense. The young people killed by the gun looked like a useless act of desperation. They ceased believing that God was with them but God said that he would make dry bones live.

The mighty apartheid machine has collapsed and the new multi-racial democratic society has begun. And not only did God make that system collapse but he gave us an extra-ordinary leader with the name of Nelson Mandela. It is a sign that tells me that nothing is impossible with God; that God was ready to break into human history in the form of the spirit of life.

God is ready to help us to break out of our limiting systems and framework which tell us that we can do nothing, and get into a world outside so that we can discover a new solution; new ways of working out our problems and new ways of finding peace and justice in the world.

Greenbelt was formed in 1974 by a young musician James Holloway when he managed to acquire a caravan, a bit of scaffolding and a damp field in East Anglia. Some 2,000 turned up on that first weekend in which 50 acts strutted their stuff.

The festival thereafter took on bigger venues, bigger ideas and bigger acts and, even though Christ was always going to remain the main focus of devotion, it was soon clear that this did not mean drippy, tambourine-banging Sunday School music, which had emptied the Sunday Schools years ago, but raw, often pulsating rock 'n' roll which was both going to make the spirits soar and the kidneys chime. Hiding their lights under bushels was not going to be a part of the strategy. Musicians were going to praise God but everyone was going to have a damned good time while they were at it.

We heard from one fine musician whose other main claim to fame was that he had once been a dope-smoking hippy actor before he was eaten by The Blob. We heard Bryn Haworth bringing the very night alive with 'We're All One' and we heard Adrian Snell present his important work *The Passion*. An unknown U2 turned up one Saturday night, performing a highly charged set a little before they became a major musical world force and there was also the immaculate professionalism of Sir Cliff of the Richard, a man who has carried the Christian torch with great dignity in the generally seedy and fallen world of rock 'n' roll.

This being England, many were the Greenbelt weekends when it poured with rain and we struggled around the site up to our arm-pits in mud, although I well remember fighting my way through a near hurricane across a deserted field late one night only to come across a gang of about twenty all holding one another and singing and dancing about like a gang of demented Mexican jumping beans.

Perhaps the unique triumph of Greenbelt is that it has created a culture of gentleness and innocence in which children always enjoy themselves and you always feel safe and unthreatened, which is not always the case when you are surrounded by the young these days. There is no alcohol for sale on the site – although it is not banned – and there is almost never any violence or crime. One man did manage to fall down one of the famous loos and wrote to the Greenbelt committee demanding damages but they wrote back rejecting his claim, pointing out that he didn't have a leg to stand on.

On another rainy, cold weekend a woman the size of a Baptist chapel was taken to the Red Cross tent suffering from hypothermia. Some twenty men were brought in to give her the rub-down of her life and all the next day she was to be seen wandering around with a huge smile on her face like some lifelong sinner who had just been told that there was no hell.

'Greenbelt stands in the market place declaring that life need not be spent in despair or treated as a long meander towards the grave,' said Stewart Henderson.

The Festival affirms that life is given to man by a God who loves, cares and cherishes each human being. We say that God is the very reason for life and that artistic creativity is a free gift given to the individual for the purpose of communal expression of exhortation to him. The God who created melody, perfect pitch, semi tones, quarter tones, rhythm, scan, metre, movement and so on wishes these forms of expression to be used as a means of enjoyment and to give spiritual understanding to life. God has all the best plans and a Festival called Greenbelt is one of them.

Let's stand and declare our faith.

It is not true that we must accept inhumanity and discrimination, death and destruction. But we believe that God's word is true and I may have life and have it in all fullness.

It is not true that we have to wait for those who are especially gifted or qualified before we can do anything. You young people shall see visions and your old folk shall dream dreams.

It is not true that everything we hear from the mouths of experts is to be believed. But we believe that God's word is true.

It is not true that the great dance of creation has to come to an end in the valley of dry bones.

We pray for the brokenness of the earth: in a world that forever seems at war we pray for Bosnia, Somalia and Rwanda, along with those war zones that have slipped off our news bulletins and out of our minds. We cry out for all the people in East Timor and all those where human rights are violated. When thousands in Africa still starve we cry out against economic systems which make it more cost effective to destroy food rather than give it away. When it seems too big a problem and too far away we cry out for the wisdom to know what to do. We pray for those with faith and those with no faith. We bring you the brokenness of our community where the gap between rich and poor opens wider. We bring to you those people without homes whom we pass every day. Help us bring healing to our own neighbourhoods and we also pray for the shattered community of the Nine O'Clock Service in Sheffield, asking that God would mend broken hearts with justice, love and mercy. Take our church and transform it. We bring you our indifference – take it from us. Let anger and love disturb and reshape us. We can be made whole, renewed by your breath and help. We are the body of Christ: the Spirit is the source of all connectedness in love. Let us greet those around us.

Swallows still kept spinning above the field as leaders in each group of this huge congregation got up to get the cup of wine and roll of bread. The bread and wine were passed around the circles as those ragged barbed wire and Coca-Cola crosses came floating down the grassy slopes.

This is the table where we meet the living God: a love undescribable and beyond our imagining yet closer than our own breath. This is where we meet the risen Christ, flesh of our flesh, bone of our bone. This is the living God made new for us in bread and wine.

The bread was eaten and the wine drunk.

Our hands are empty, our hearts are full of wrong things, we are not fit to pick up the crumbs around your table. Bring life to our tired old bones. Here is your Lord coming to you with bread and wine. This is my body, It was broken for you. Do this in remembrance of me.

A silence swept around and around the worshipping slopes which ended with the wail of a saxophone and the singing of 'Freedom is Coming'. Unwinding snakes of conga dancing began turning here and there, reminding you that dancing is what they like the best, worshipping God with the whole of their bodies. No dry bones in Greenbelt '95. Dem bones dem bones they were all a'dancing.

Greenbelt is the best argument I know which proves that the strangest triumph of Christianity is that it actually works.

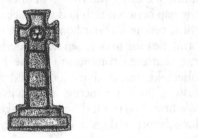

SEVEN

Palace of the Ice Queen

TWO RED ADMIRAL butterflies went tumbling across the road, locked together in an energetic display of fluttering aerobatics as the huge guns kept spitting out water in rising loops over the dripping crops. But, as the pilgrim eyes lifted higher, there was nothing but sky, layer upon layer of sky, all piled up on top of one another above the flatlands of these Fens which were so perfectly flat that a whole army of angels may have once been commanded by the Archangel Michael himself to each take up an iron and erase every crease and hillock in sight.

Some of the towns had been built as crowns on the odd 'island' in this wilderness of flatness but mostly it all looks like one of these snapshots that we always took with our Box Brownies when we were kids: a huge expanse of glimmering grey light supported by the tiniest sliver of land with someone's forehead somewhere in the middle. But even this sliver of land is unlike any other, you soon discover, since it is criss-crossed by a watery geometry of rivers and huge drains. There's the 20-mile-long Hundred Foot and the Forty Foot running directly across the land and straight into the sky in slash-straight lines. But there are curling rivers too with their sluggish brown water catching the light until it seems that the whole of this dark, peaty land has veins which are both crooked and straight, running this way and that, in glittering hoops and lines of silvery brown. Just occasionally the flatness is broken up by a line of poplars trembling in the breeze.

Many of the Fen roads run along the sides of the drains and turning off them and out into the crops are lots of concrete tracks known as droves. These droves will be covered with mud in the coming autumn but today they are still warm and dusty; still waiting for that huge deluge of rain which does not quite seem to want to happen. When cars run across the droves the dust gets trapped in their wheels like swirling brown ghosts struggling to escape. There are always those errant Fen winds

71

too – known as Fen blows – which can pick up the dust off a surface of a single field and start whirling it around like a mini-tornado that we're always seeing tearing apart Florida on the television news.

There is a whole world buried beneath the black peat of the Fens and they say that, on some nights, you can hear Roman centurions marching along the old roads that lie buried here. Or else you can hear the chanting of the old monks at Ramsey Abbey or even, if your luck is really out, come face to face with some massive marauding Viking with an axe in hand and about to halve your skull. They dug up the skeleton of a whole elephant at Chatteris and how he got all the way down there no one knows for sure.

But what we do know for sure is that this was a dark, medieval Waterworld; a place of disease, rheumatism and chronic arthritis. We know that it was once a harsh place of cock fights, public floggings and tread-mills inhabited by an ignorant, superstitious people who used to make leg garters out of eels to ward off rheumatism or put live spiders in bags around their necks to ward off plague or use the hands of corpses to rub against skin diseases.

Apart from the 'islands' this whole area was covered by water and, when they began draining this 'land of musty ague and unwholesome swamp', the locals fought the authorities with such ferocity that they became known as Fen Tigers. Fen folk were also known as Yellow Bellies because they lived like frogs and the men who walked on stilts in the marshes were known as Cambridgeshire Camels.

But not even the Fen Tigers could put a stop to the drainage in the end as the likes of Oliver Cromwell brought in hundreds of prisoners from Scotland who, with wheelbarrow and shovel, dug out huge areas so that they could control rivers and reduce flooding until it finally became as we see it today; a huge flatland holding up many layers of grey sky where you almost feel yourself spreading your legs to steady yourself since at times it actually does feel as if you are at sea as you look up and around you into the misty eyes of all these shifting skies.

And then it appeared like some strange portent in all these shifting skies, rising up beneath some curling rain clouds like a lighthouse of hope set in the midst of this flat sea of pain; the Mother Church of the Fens, Ely Cathedral.

Ely was another of those 'islands' out here – thought to be once known as Eel Island – but today it is a lively and unusual collection of medieval gateways, narrow streets with lots of shops and ancient buildings scattered around the skirts of the awesome cathedral.

I stopped first to have a quick look around the cemetery in St Mary's Church. This one, I soon discovered, was once notorious for body-snatchers who would then cart the bodies off to nearby Cambridge University to be sliced up in medical research. Indeed the sexton at the time was fingered as the source of such information and it was reported that he finally confessed to receiving £10 for every successful exhumation.

Body-snatching became such a widespread racket that all sorts of devices were introduced into the cemeteries, in the form of heavy slabs and iron railings, to deter them. Four bodies were said to have been dug up one night in this cemetery alone actually leading to riots of outraged protest in Ely.

It's strange how people drift into the oddest professions when you come to think about it. Of my own school class one is a book-maker, another a funeral director, another a motor bike racing champion and three are languishing for a long time yet in prison. But in the past ten years or so I have almost become a professional pilgrim finding myself time and again wandering from holy shrine to holy shrine or else flogging up some steep mountain or tramping over cold stones in my bare feet usually for the purposes of a book, a television programme or a newspaper series.

And do you actually get paid for that? One man once asked me with his eyebrows rising into his hairline when I told him what I did for a living. Well, sometimes.

Almost every Easter I find myself girding up my loins to go on some improbable pilgrimage or other, and my career being such as it is I now calculate that I've long rubbed the slate clean of all my past sins and furthermore I could probably now keep sinning with impunity – and certainly with no prospect of any particularly severe punishment in the afterlife – until I drop.

During my various pilgrimages I have also acquired – along with blistered feet and sore legs – a truly vast pile of useless knowledge about such as the foibles of medieval saints or the strengths and weaknesses of various styles of church architecture. But I have also developed what some might describe as an unhealthy obsession with cemeteries, remembering there and then in Ely that they also once had such an awful problem with body-snatching in Glasnevin cemetery in Dublin that they built fortified walls with high turrets around the cemetery, which have remained there to this day. They also turned huge guard dogs loose at night inside the grounds in the quiet hope that they would take a big bite out of any body-snatchers who managed to scale those fortified walls. Unfortunately those same guard dogs took a big bite out of the cemetery superintendent and, no sooner had they bandaged him up, he ordered all the dogs to be put down.

My obsession with cemeteries is not nearly as bad as that of another man whom I once met – in a cemetery, as it happened. He explained that he even liked to spend his holidays in cemeteries and only the previous year had gone to Greece where a friend had asked him to visit a relative's grave in Salonika to check it out. Not only did he agree to do that with the greatest of pleasure – Greek cemeteries are lovely, scrubbed places with nice photos of the deceased on many of the graves – but he also ended up taking a flask of tea and his sandwiches down to eat with the gravediggers each day of his hols because he found them extremely congenial company. Greek gravediggers are the most marvellous conversationalists, he insisted with great relish; certainly better company than the *Sun*-reading lager louts who now litter most Greek beaches.

I couldn't have agreed more. Where better, I have often wondered, to spend a happy and recreational few hours than being in an overgrown cemetery while inspecting the inscriptions on tombstones amidst all those hovering stone angels? It's always best to be alone when walking around them and even better if it is raining. The raindrops falling off the overhanging branches seem like tears, almost as if the trees are trying to speak to you from the depths of their breaking hearts. Everywhere you turn in the hissing, failing light there is ivy clawing at the sides of the tombs and generally a robin will come and chirp at you, doubtless hoping that you are going to produce a shovel and dig him some big, fat worms. Robins love cemeteries too.

But you always feel a certain kind of tension while you're in them, a bit like a vibrating tuning fork, which can also take the form of an extreme nervousness; a kind of formless panic that you are about to miss the bus yet again. This panic is mirrored in the tense brawling of the plant life all around you: the cow parsley battling with the nettles, the ferns in hand-to-hand combat with the cowslip and the brambles trying to throttle the very life out of the laurel. Nettles are terrific growers in cemeteries because they thrive on the phosphates of human bones.

Oh to be sure it is always incandescently lovely being cast adrift in an overgrown cemetery on a rainy day. The cemetery in St Tropez has a beautiful position on a headland overlooking the sea and the IRA plot in Milltown, Belfast, is always unfailingly interesting too. The most dramatically atmospheric cemetery I have ever wandered is Montmartre in Paris with whole avenues of huge Gothic tombs where, in some, you can actually see the coffins with the woodworm and verdigris on their fittings, all nestling down on the shelves like a left-luggage office. But the oddest feature of Montmartre is the hundreds of wild cats who slip around behind the tombs, even giving birth inside some and hissing at you if you dare to move too close.

But my favourite cemetery – the cemetery of cemeteries – has to be Highgate in North London, where some 166,000 bodies have been buried in 51,000 graves. A few are the lonely forgotten graves of paupers but many of the tombs are fabulous creations such as might have been ordered for a Ming Emperor or Egyptian Pharaoh.

Turn left along here and we come to the Egyptian Avenue of the Dead; a Gothic alleyway where Radclyffe Hall, the lesbian novelist, is buried with her first lover, the wealthy Mabel Batten. Just around the corner is the vandalized and plundered tomb of F. W. Woolworth who, in his early days here, used to have his dress shirt changed once a week by his grief-stricken widow. He always loved to have a crisp, clean shirt, she explained to bemused relatives and friends.

Just up the way is the extravagant tomb of Julius Beer who once owned the *Observer* newspaper. A Victorian riot in indulgence it cost more than £2m. to build and was decorated in gold leaf, being modelled on the world's oldest tomb, that of King Mausolus of Greece. Behind those dripping trees is the grave of Charles Dickens and then there is that of the poet, Gabriel Rosetti, the writer George Eliot and the last of the bare-fisted fighters, Tom Sayers. Over the road a way lies Karl Marx where, almost daily, hordes of green-jacketed Chinese come to lay flowers on the old earth-shaker's grave. Others make a similar pilgrimage merely to deface it.

In one grave there is a man who shot himself in the foot. Here lies the ashes of a woman who incinerated herself when she set her ballgown alight. This man studied the movements of tides and beneath that brambled heap lies the first man to discover electricity. They are all here, the famous and the unknown, the rich and the poor, all dreaming their dead dreams beneath this stunning backdrop of sorrowing yew and the fluffy waterfalls of old man's beard.

Everyone should visit and come to enjoy these sprawling poems gone wild, I've long thought. They are serene places of death where you can moon around while trying to pick up new insights into life. Indeed everyone should adopt one of their very own where they can watch the squirrels and the changing seasons; where they can monitor the new graves and note who is still being remembered with the love of fresh flowers.

One quiet morning in spring they might even find, if they were very lucky, a shy stammering of violets sitting beneath some old Celtic cross, mysterious in its mysticism. Or else they might come across an angel so beautifully and carefully carved it might be about to take flight. But the real value of a visit to an old cemetery is that it both reminds you that life is but a short journey while also bringing you that bit closer to an understanding and acceptance of the clear dark shadow which falls over us all.

And there was, at the minute, another clear dark shadow hanging over me since I was standing in Ely Cathedral, home of Etheldreda, that strange and legendary queen of ice. I always, without fail, feel her presence when I step into this vast, shadowy place since the spirit of this ice queen still lives on and broods here, touching each and every pilgrim with her iciness and remoteness, her piety and inaccessibility, her discipline and pride.

You pick up on these unfashionable and unusual qualities when you look up and along the huge length and emptiness of the Norman nave whose striking height is also emphasized by its narrowness. They are also there in the bare, flag-stoned floors and the absence of any bright primary colours. Everything is the dull colour of old stone; only cold, thick shadows move around inside here. You can even see it in the old Victorian boilers dotted around the sides of the nave which, you are told by the guide and believe implicitly, cost a fortune to run and do not heat much at all.

I once attended a morning service here at Easter and even though we were all huddled together in the choir stalls with overcoats, scarves and winter long johns – they *told* us to come well wrapped up – I would have been warmer and a lot happier sitting on top of the North Pole. We chattered and shivered and then chattered and shivered some more. Even the choir boys were wearing gloves and turning blue around the gills.

But let us never forget that we were in the courtyard of Etheldreda the ice queen, that singular lady who founded this great thing in the Fens some thirteen centuries ago. It would be possible to wander this place on your hands and knees for a whole year but you would not find a single trace of human sensuality or frailty. Even the darkness of many of the corners seems darker than other similar corners you have known as you can see when you light a candle here which seems to glow with an unreal vivacity.

Etheldreda was a woman of great piety who only ever washed in cold water and prayed almost constantly. Even when she was dying an extremely nasty death from cancer of the throat she delighted in her pain but my hunch is that, despite all this, she was an extremely attractive woman since she was wooed by some of the most powerful and eligible princes of the time. But unfortunately for these princes Etheldreda did not believe in sex either before or after marriage and, in fact, it was because of her icy frigidity that this cathedral was built.

Her virginity actually survived two marriages: one to Tondbert, a local prince in 652 and, after he died, to Prince Egfrid of Northumbria. Neither of them consummated the marriage in bed and indeed within hours of marrying Egfrid, far from asking for a honeymoon in Barbados, she was demanding to be allowed to go into a convent. As it happened he gave way on this, probably out of sheer exasperation but he later came to regret his decision, once pursuing her, complete with army, right across Northumbria where again her virginity remained intact since she took refuge on a promontory and was saved by a sudden flood. Damp, dispirited and not a little frustrated, Egfrid decided

78

that this was a sign from heaven that he would never have her so he abandoned the chase and went home.

Etheldreda finally fetched up here in Ely where she founded a double monastery for monks and nuns, becoming its first abbess and, perhaps predictably, this proto-feminist only then spoke to the monks through a window.

Years after she died her body was exhumed and found to be free of any form of corruption and this place became a famous centre for medieval pilgrimage. You can still look out over the surrounding Fens and picture those early pilgrims making their way here by boat or picking their way through the secret pathways in the marsh. Then they would have filed in through that door there, goggle-eyed and cap in hand, as they looked up and around this towering place which they found so shocking and inspirational.

This cathedral has been sacked by the Danes, destroyed and squatted in by Cromwell's troops, shaken by storms, ravaged by decay and chewn away by death-watch beetles. 'Some of it is so ancient and totters so much with every gust of wind and looks so like decay,' Daniel Defoe wrote of Ely in 1720 'that whenever it does fall, all that 'tis likely will be thought strange in it, will be that it didn't fall a hundred years sooner.'

But it didn't fall – even if the tower did once – although it nearly did close some ten years back since almost every part of it had fallen into such a state of disrepair. Faced with mounting costs and no financial reserves the cathedral decided to charge an entrance fee of £1.60p, the first in the country to do so. With 200,000 visitors a year the average contribution had been 32p a head, which effectively meant that they were subsidizing each visitor.

This new charge outraged some but it did turn the fortunes of the place around and made their future safe. Before the admission charges they could barely pay the wage bill and with no staff just could not have opened the doors. Even the roof of one of the canons had fallen in and he was living under canvas. But soon they moved into a small surplus. There was also a large refund of VAT since, as yet, worship is zero-rated.

There have been lots of letters of complaint about the charges, which have all received detailed replies. A canon is still called to the west door by people complaining but, on hearing the cathedral's problems, they always pay up. There is no charge on Sundays and people do now spend longer in the cathedral.

But what value it is to be able to wander down the ice queen's amazing, long nave and then gaze up at the soaring oak crown of her octagon tower – two hundred tons of wood, lead and glass which seems to be just floating up there like some visiting medieval flying saucer. Light pours through the windows on all eight sides and indeed through those of the lantern on the top, framing and holding the life-size wooden carving of Christ in some new and miraculous crucifixion, involving many horizontal and upright beams of constantly moving light.

The pilgrim can then go and marvel at the colours in the Stained Glass Museum or sit in the small explosions of light and the intricate stone carvings of Cambridgeshire clunch in the Lady Chapel. Here he can pick up intimations of the ice queen's purity in an atmosphere which has been hallowed by centuries of believing prayer. Here his very soul can reach out and take her by the hand.

The whole building gives you a sense of what it feels like to be disciplined, prayerful and strong in Christ. For this is the home of Etheldreda still . . . ice queen, virgin, saint.

The skies opened up and it poured down with rain, emptying relentlessly and without pause, for hour after hour, on the orange rooftops of this tiny Norfolk village, scattered around a cobbled centre. This rain rained on everything, the drops hitting the puddles in tiny silver javelins, sliding down the rooftops on their backsides and gurgling merrily in the drainpipes before spilling out over the sloping cobbled roads sometimes making it into the gutters and at others building up into deep pools which began spelling f-l-o-o-d. A man dashed along the pavement with one hand holding the lapels of his jacket together as his other held up a newspaper over his head in the form of an umbrella.

It rained on Sharon's Pantry and the Sue Ryder Shop and the Swallows Restaurant. It rained on the Russian Orthodox Church in the old railway station and on the Sisters of Mercy in their little cottage up the hill. It rained on the old court room which has now been turned into a museum complete with a prisoner's lock-up with a barred grille. In 1833 a man was sentenced to seven years transportation for stealing six hens, it said on the wall. A five-year-old was also imprisoned for seven days for stealing a box. It rained too on the Old Bakehouse and The Craft Shop. 'If you are feeling pale and wan then pray you have no fear,' it said on a tea-cloth in the Craft Shop's window. 'These Norfolk monks and Norfolk punch will bring you health and cheer. This ruby draught, an ancient brew, one sip will bring the reflection that Norfolk punch is good for you and that's without exception.'

The grounds of the old ruined abbey were not exempt from the rain either with grass already thickening up into a lush green after being brown and dead for so long. It poured down on the lonely arch, which is all that's left of the old abbey, and on the nearby Pack Horse Bridge over the tiny stream which had become swollen and giddy with new life as it chased around the bends in the gently hissing glade. The rain also pattered loudly on the greenhouse roof on the other side of the grounds which, in turn, protected the fat red bunches of tomatoes below. It rained too on the old house where several workmen were taking shelter beneath some scaffolding, waiting for a break in the rain which never came. A cat wandered across the grass looking around before stopping for a long stretch, unconcerned, it would seem, by this appalling wet weather.

A charabanc pulled up in the car park near the Black Lion Hotel and around thirty people spilled out. They were anorak'd and umbrella'd, wellingtoned and sou'westered, mackintoshed and cagouled; all now forming an untidy but good-tempered queue behind a large wooden monstrance shouldered by four men before moving off, in a long, splashy crocodile, into the rain-swept countryside. *Hail Mary, full of grace, the Lord is with thee* . . . Cold fingers ran through the beads of damp rosaries and raindrops chased one another off the ends of pilgrim noses. Occasionally they stopped in the brambled lane next to a fast brown stream as the rain kept coming. *Blessed art thou among women and blessed is* . . .

The Anglican shrine here in Walsingham – otherwise known as England's Nazareth – was full of flickering candles and the cloying smells of burning incense and expensive rain-coats. This is a strange, rabbit warren of a building with no less than fifteen separate chapels scattered around a high altar and a holy well. The sick, the lame and the handicapped have all struggled to this well, seeking out the healing powers of the water but, just now, the well was locked and a man was taking his daughter around and explaining what's what. 'Please God help our sister and her heart problem,' it has tacked on the prayer requests. 'Pray for Martin Oswald, a joyful pilgrim for 60 years.'

This shrine is a shadowy place with very little natural light although there were hundreds of guttering candles in almost every corner. Outside in the gardens there was a Way of the Cross complete with all the stations and a replica of Calvary. Fallen apples, glistening with the rain, lay on the grass near a wall; a few had gone rotten and a few more were being drilled by the last of the summer wasps. There was a sudden and unex-pected peal of laughter from one of the chapels. Near the door was a newspaper with a headline which took you straight back out into the ubiquitous and growing savagery of the modern world. BOYS, 10, HELD OVER DEATH OF A WOMAN. The boys had dropped a lump of concrete off some high-rise flats on top of this poor woman and you looked away, suddenly feeling short of breath, your mind fumbling badly, unsure what or who you were now supposed to pray for.

About a mile outside the town that damp crocodile of pil-grims had now reached the Roman Catholic Slipper Chapel where it broke up and they were making little jokes about Noah and the flood as they made their way to the restaurant for a warm, reviving cup of tea. They were from Liverpool and Ponte-fract and you suspected that each of them had drunk thousands, if not millions, of such warm, reviving cups of tea in their life-times.

The flowers had all long fallen off the hollyhocks in the garden borders and there was a brisk trade in religious icons in the gift shop. Soon everyone would be gathering in the modern circular Chapel of Reconciliation at the other end of the grounds for a service of prayer and worship. A hand pulled back a lace curtain in one of the cottages and a face looked up dismally with a down-turned mouth at the continuing rain.

But the rain did stop pouring on this Nazareth of England some hours later and, with the sun trying to break through the mists, a great and thrilling rainbow formed over the outlying fields. They say that a rainbow is made by light refracting at different wavelengths through millions of raindrops.

I say that the rainbow is made from the spirit of truth; it is an earnest of God's firm promise that he will not flood the world again; the gorgeous colours are also the colours of Christ's throne from which he will one day soon step down and reclaim the leadership of all the tribes of his lost and fallen people.

EIGHT

Dracula's Town

THE WIND KEPT whipping big, black clouds across the roof of the sky as the odd burst of sunshine swept across the purple and mauve moorland. Drystone walls cut the countryside into wonky squares and the twisting lanes were full of whispers of the coming autumn with all sorts of damp, musty smells hanging themselves up to dry in the crystal air. Stone barns sat quietly at the bottom of valleys and, high on the crests of the hills, I kept coming across broken stone crosses. At almost every bend in the road sheep, with no discernible sense of the Highway Code, stumbled out in front of speeding cars as if hoping to end it all there and then.

A posse of ducks bobbed along a muddy stream in the next valley. Other clearer streams gushed out of gullies on high and joined the ones below. Skylarks gossiped and car horns beeped warnings at the suicidal sheep.

I had come to the Yorkshire Dales, the roof of England, to begin the final legs of my summer pilgrimage. But, with autumn now threatening to foreclose on the land, the summer had clearly run out of puff and already a few of the leaves had begun falling on to the hurrying streams which they rode like small speeding coracles. These are the first leaves to fall but they don't just fall for a week or two; they will now fall at different times and keep on falling right up to Christmas. Fires were burning in some parts of the moorland where game-keepers were burning off the old heather to provide new growth for the grouse.

You could sing songs of love to the Dales all year long. The Dales are freedom and high winds; they are a sudden longing in the night and an unexpected, light kiss when you awake. There's a solitude and a purity of passion in those fells . . . and danger too. On some days all the winds of the land come fighting and brawling with one another over those iron-jawed crags but, on others, nothing moves in the silent stillness of these

moors and all that you can hear is the crumbling music of your breaking heart.

The Dales, I came to learn, had actually been wrested from the wilderness by monks, and their fingerprints can still be seen everywhere to this day. The monks were great walkers and all those ragged stone crosses you can find squatting around almost everywhere marked out the lines between those old great abbeys like Whitby, Gisborough, Byland and Rievaulx. These same abbeys are broken ruins now but, back in the twelfth century, almost a third of the moors was directly under monastic control.

The monks first came here to escape from what they perceived as the growing spiritual corruption of society, seeking somewhere among these thorns and swamps to conduct their life of one long secret prayer. They built the abbeys then drained the swamps and irrigated the land. They took away the wilderness forever, first introducing sheep here and selling the wool in Europe. Monks sculpted out all those lanes and trackways; they built the stone bridges and all those drystone walls to settle disputes over land. They tilled the fields and even planted millions of daffodil bulbs which still explode into whole shimmering acres of brilliant yellow in the spring.

Even as you cross the Dales beneath those whipped clouds, past stone crosses and ruined Abbeys, you are always mindful that those monks first came to this wilderness the better to honour and praise God. You also become mindful that the religious roots of England often go far deeper than you can ever quite see or possibly imagine; that the very rain here is much like the blood of Christ, forever recycling itself through cloud and evaporation, bringing up crop after crop, year after year, in well-tuned and eternal cycles of resurrection and death.

It was on the Dales, in the village of Hawes in Wensleydale, that I met, a few years back, one of the most eccentric Christians that I have ever come across. Kit Calvert was his name, a rough and ready Yorkshireman who was spending all his time translating the Bible into Yorkshire dialect: 'Now it cam about; them days at Caesar A'gustus gav oot an order . . .'

When I called at his home he was wearing a battered trilby which he stuck on his head as soon as he got out of bed, his boots were unlaced, his clay pipe in his mouth upside down, his braces broken and his gritty face in need of a shave. He was 76 and his dog three-legged. On the wall a good old Yorkshire adage: 'Hear all, see all, say nowt.'

We chatted about his small bookshop where, if you wanted a book, you just left your money in a church collection plate – 'I just opens the shops and leaves it' – and then about his enthusiasm for dialect. 'Jesus spoke dialect you know.' Kit was a committed Christian, he said, and I asked him how he became one.

'Better put pipe away for this,' he said, placing it carefully on the mantelpiece when, lo and behold, he launched into one of the strangest accounts of a personal conversion that I have ever heard. It lasted a good hour, complete with sound effects and animal noises and I had a strong suspicion that he had told it once or twice before. Here, anyway, are the bones of Kit's own Damascus road conversion.

When he was much younger than he was today he had saved up all his money to buy a cow. He wanted to enter this cow into a beauty competition but it had a nasty blemish so he got a vet 'down with the drink' to operate on this blemish. The long and short of it was that this cow got blood poisoning because of this vet's drunken habits and dirty needles and duly began pegging out. At this point in the narrative Kit proceeded to imitate the painful, blood-poisoned mooings of this cow.

At the time of the cow's illness he was an agnostic but, in desperation, he then went down to the hay shed and slumped to his knees next to said cow. 'Oh Lord take her out of her misery or make her better,' he pleaded with his arms raised. 'Make her better and I'll follow you.'

Well the cow got better – more sound effects of a recovering, happy cow – and, from that day on, Kit became a devoted and faithful servant of the Lord.

Whitby is an indecently attractive fishing town scattered down over cliff and cove around the mouth of the River Esk as it hurries down a deep valley and under a viaduct before debouching into the sea. The higgledy-piggledy houses seem to have been slung everywhere they could find any room without too much thought for civic planning, with lots of pubs jostling with shops and many gulls cruising the ozone keeping their yellow eyes primed for anything interesting to eat that may be dropped by the fishermen as they unload their catches on the foul-smelling pier. The town once used to be a large and active centre of the herring industry before the herring upped sticks and went somewhere else – as herring are prone to do.

It was also once a centre for the whaling industry still commemorated by an arch of whale jawbones at the end of East Terrace. Scoresby, the man who invented the crow's nest, sailed out of here and the Whitby street lamps were once fuelled with whale oil.

The dominant feature of the town is the ruined Whitby Abbey which sits on a flat headland looking out over all as serenely as an old and down-at-heel African chieftain watching his gathered tribe performing their dances to his eternal glory. The abbey is not too ruined as ruins go since you can still see much of its original shape even if the roof has long since collapsed and there are no what estate agents are pleased to call mod cons. The guide book, with the usual sort of rhetorical flourish that you find in guide books, calls the abbey 'a burial-place of kings, repository of relics and training ground for a galaxy of saints'.

We do know that the abbey was founded by Hilda in 657 who also gave shelter to Caedmon, the famous composer of English sacred songs. Then it was sacked by the Vikings like the wondrously handled Eric Bloodaxe –

> They spread themselves over the whole country and filled all with blood and grief; they destroyed the churches and monasteries far and wide with fire and sword, leaving nothing remaining save the bare unroofed walls.

The Benedictines re-built the abbey in the eleventh century when they would also have begun taming the Yorkshire moors, many of them basing their activities on the inspirational cult of St Cuthbert, the North's most popular saint. There was little these monks couldn't build since they also erected the mighty Durham Cathedral where Cuthbert is buried.

St Mary's Church, which sits on a slope just below Whitby Abbey, might be one of the oddest that I have ever stepped inside with its rectangular nave filled with boxed pews and irregular galleries built nearly three hundred years ago from sections of ships. But the jewel in this particular church's crown is undoubtedly the three-decker pulpit in which the preacher would take up a level depending on the importance of what he had to say. Parish announcements were made from the bottom deck but sermons were always delivered from the top from where the preacher could also 'rake' every corner and member of the congregation. It was not likely that anyone could quietly nod off when he got going up there.

Whitby was amok with day-trippers and moored boats when I arrived there since it was a Saturday and the tide was out. There was a sign on the pier pointing out: THE THROWING OF MISSILES AT BOATS IS FORBIDDEN, making you wonder if it was actually permissible to throw missiles at everything else. Elsewhere along the quay and up past the shops in the narrow, cobbled alley-ways it was much the same cheerfully vulgar story of crazed seagulls and bustling pubs and hot pork and stuffing sandwiches which, when bitten, sent two lines of fat dribbling down from either end of your mouth to gather in a greasy mess all over your chin.

More charabancs pulled into the coach park disgorging yet more old people, clearly on some mystery trip as they oohed and aahed their way in dim gestures of recognition along the quay. You noticed by their slow and hunched shufflings how so many of our old people suffer from the cruelties of such as lumbago, arthritis and varicose veins. Every movement was difficult and painful for many: no longer for them the jumping about and rave dancing of youth.

I sat on a bench at the end of the harbour, looking across the mud flats at the stone Church Stairs leading up to St Mary's Church sitting marooned in a sea of wonky, blackened tombstones. (I was always worried about the reason for the sootied state of these tombstones until I found out that they had been blackened by all the coal fires here which were later outlawed by The Clean Air Act. Every chimney in pre-war Whitby belched thick black smoke, I saw from one postcard. They are still in such a bad state that the last film company to come here to make yet another version of *Dracula* brought their own tombstones.)

Way out on my left were the sands where Lewis Carroll was thought to have written much of *Alice in Wonderland*. Captain Cook also once lived in a terrace directly behind me before he sailed off and got himself into so much trouble around Tahiti, and they've put up a statue to him too. But the main focus of interest in Whitby today must be on the large and red-haired writer Bram Stoker since it was here in an apartment in 6 Royal Crescent late last century that he began writing his famous book *Dracula*.

The heroines of the book, Mina and her friend Lucy, were spending their summer holidays in East Crescent in Whitby and it was in No 7 East Crescent that a lawyer was engaged by Count Dracula to handle the import of his strange cargo from Transylvania, to wit 'fifty cases of common earth'. The two girls were thoroughly enjoying their holiday until a bat flitted into the action rather like the bats that still flit around the spire of St Mary's Church in the evenings. Normality quickly returned but Mina saw how pale and listless her friend had become.

Then in that churchyard over there Lucy, when looking for her friend, saw a white figure 'with what looked like something dark bending over her'. In the setting sun in the windows of St Mary's, Lucy also saw 'his red eyes again'. From the nearby railway station Count Dracula was thought to have left for St Pancras concealed inside one of the cases of 'common earth'.

The Russian schooner *Demeter* crashed against the Tate Hill Pier directly over there in a storm with the dead captain lashed to the wheel and the ship deserted. A huge black dog leaped off the stricken ship and disappeared into those alleys where 'the churchyard hangs over the laneway to the East Pier'. Directly across the mudflats Mina ran up the 199 stone steps of the Church Stairs where she saw Lucy sitting with 'something long and black beside her'. In the cemetery itself, somewhere amidst all those wonky black tombstones and whirling bats, Dracula, the dread Count of the un-Dead, took refuge in the unhallowed grave of a suicide who had been buried as an 'accidental death'. (There is no record of such a grave although there is Caedmon's

Cross where the rather less lurid composer of sacred songs actually is buried.)

'The funeral of the poor sea-captain was most touching', Bram Stoker wrote in *Dracula*.

> Every boat in the harbour seemed to be there, and the coffin was carried by captains all the way from Tate Hill Pier up to the Churchyard. We went to our old seat whilst the cortege of boats went up the river to the viaduct and came down again. We had a lovely view and saw the procession nearly all the way.

And so, just by sitting here on a harbour bench, amidst the old day-trippers and smell of chips, it is possible to see, in one single sweep of a view, the early framework of this influential book which has never been out of print since Bram Stoker's death in 1912 and has been filmed more than eight times. Stoker could even have been sitting on this very bench when he wrote those words.

But surely then this town must have real and even ominous implications for every Christian in the world. There must be a real argument that Whitby is not so much another English landscape of glory but a dried-up oasis in a desert of shame since what else is *Dracula* but another of those Gothic viruses which, like *Frankenstein*, then went on to poison the bloodstream of the world's media?

In its frequent and lurid emphasis on sexual terror and cruelty; in the bloody viciousness of its violence and constant invocation of all the demonology of hell; in the way it hums with the quiet of the ordinary world before exploding into an orgy of vampires and the occult, not only will the book *Dracula* have done much to undermine the Christian confidence of nineteenth-century England but it will also have set up a virulent blood-line directly down into the body of our modern media. Far from glorying in and celebrating the beauties of the ordinary world, far from insisting on St Paul's 'whatsoever is pure, whatsoever is lovely, whatsoever men that are of good report', the media love nothing more than dealing with sexual terror, sickening violence, incessant cruelty and the whole vampiric world of the occult and nightmare.

It would be difficult to locate almost any section of our modern media free from such evil obsessions and it could well be that popular and influential books like *Dracula* came to legitimize and even sanctify such obsessions. Here in Whitby yet another virus was hatched which then broke free and joined with the others in poisoning and laying low the very world.

It is probably worth reminding ourselves again that *Dracula* is a work of the imagination; a total fiction. Count Dracula of the un-Dead never existed and the story goes that Bram Stoker conceived him in a bad dream after a supper of Whitby crab. But Dracula is no less dangerous for that and his spirit straddles the world. He is even here next to me in today's newspaper with its round-up of the world's violence, hate and cruelty. He is there in the details of the evidence against Rosemary West, accused of 10 murders of young girls in Winchester Crown Court; he is there in the same newspaper with the wife-killer sent to Broadmoor and there again in all the details of yet another sex trial and yet again in yet another report of yet another murdered woman found buried in a back garden.

For all this is the spirit of Dracula; the spirit which dwells on and feeds on horror, pain, violence and cruelty; the spirit of evil, pure and simple.

But even as I sat there on that bench making notes in Whitby harbour with a light autumnal sun on my head, just as I suppose Bram Stoker might have done before me, I had to admit that I would never really know quite what contribution Stoker had made to the present fallen world, particularly as there were clearly lots of other pens of his ilk. We can never really expose exact sources of evil because evil never works like that; evil always comes in the guise of good and unfailingly insists that it is not there.

There was one thing we could all be sure of however, and that is that no mere stake hammered through his heart was going to stop Dracula now. Not only did his fanged spirit live on throughout the world and our global media but he was even being presented here in Whitby as a real person, doubtless to beef up the tourist trade in much the same way as the monks of old often appropriated saint's 'relics' or a part of the 'true cross' to beef up the pilgrim trade.

Right next to the Fish Pier they have a museum called The Dracula Experience and, after forking out a few pounds, I went into it, finding that it was all set out in a series of dark corridors with each of the exhibits triggered by an infra-red beam which was broken as you walked through.

Thus I came across a trembling, severed hand and heard distant screams and stood in front of a mock-up of the Russian schooner *Demeter* with the dead captain lashed to the wheel and the big, black dog escaping on to the shore. But it was only while looking at another of the exhibits that I became aware of someone moving about in the darkness at the end of the corridor and this someone was definitely not a dummy. Whatever he was he made me really agitated and I wasn't sure whether to hit him with my carrier bag full of shopping or simply make a run for it when he swooped past me with a swoosh of his cape and a soft hiss of his fanged teeth.

That was it; that was it. I triggered the rest of the exhibits before I got to them by swinging my carrier bag through the infra red beam in front of me and then went crashing out through the back door of the place like some drunk being thrown out through the swing doors of a Wild West saloon.

The fanged figure, I discovered later, was an actor hired to put the wind up poor saps like me. These people; they really are going to be the death of us all.

NINE

The Shadow of Cuthbert

THE SUMMER HAD finally drifted to an end and it was one long
story of thick mists and falling leaves as this pilgrim began
looking for an end to his pilgrimage by wandering aimlessly
across the roof of England, roaming the huge and shifting
continents of his morning dreams.

Those falling leaves seemed to be getting everywhere, drifting
across the roads and lanes in great rattling storms before settling
down for a while and then getting disturbed by the draughts of
passing cars which made them all leap up into yet more small
rattling storms. The leaves built up in greasy, rotten piles in
corners of fields or else did their level best to block up the drains
and gutters or stop the trains again. Everywhere people were
sweeping up these leaves in their gardens and then lighting
smoky bonfires which never quite seemed to want to light. Fat
red apples also fell in rifle-shots in these gardens and, when the
sun was out, big daddy-long-legs gathered in sunny porches
doing whatever bid daddy-long-legs do in sunny porches. Swallows were also gathering in long lines of musical notes on the
telegraph wires, as if waiting for the word from The Great Con-
ductor in the Sky before the whole symphony of them broke up
into discordant swirls to fly off way down south to winter somewhere warm in the sun. Lucky old swallows.

Early one autumnal morning in Cumbria I sat on a stone
wall with a cup of hot coffee in my hands watching a river
gurgling through the mists in front of me and noting the dew-
jewelled cobwebs pegged out on the gnarled, arthritic branches
of the bushes when I also noticed that the small yellow leaves
of one tree were all falling so furiously that it was as if the tree
had decided that it simply had to shed the lot in the next half
an hour, hundreds of them drifting and shimmying down
through the air in an extravagant autumnal firework display
before settling down in a crunchy brittle carpet around the
tree's feet.

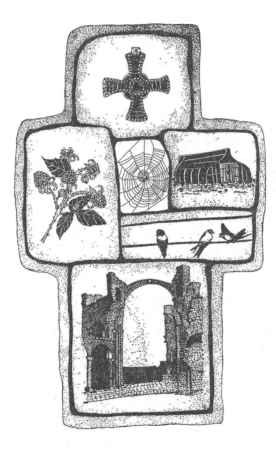

I came to Eskdale in the Lake District and over there was Hard Knot Pass. It rained warmly for a while and then the sun came out in indecisive bursts. A buzzard called, gliding through the rain mists looking around the crags for something small and furry for dinner. A packet steamer left a quay on Coniston, breaking up the glassy surface of the lake into rippling V-shapes as whiffs of exhaust steam whiffled up out of its Edwardian funnel. Quite soon the steamer disappeared into the mists as if by some trick of smoke 'n' mirrors.

You could get very lonely in some of these parts as you gaze down into the deep, secret gullies and over at vanishing boats. In fact you would have to hold your breath for a long, long time and then listen very hard before you could hear even the loudest cry of anguish down in that gorge. But where there are now just falling leaves there will soon be freezing winds and piled-up snow on unpassable roads when it will get lonelier still.

Shaggy grey Herdwick sheep wandered everywhere looking for something to eat beneath the damp leaves. It seems they will eat almost anything but daffodils. There were lunar cliffs and immense woods. As it looked now, then so too it must once have looked to those Roman boys who, a long way from their mothers and home, first built all their roads and forts out these ways.

In lonely Windermere the tourist season had long come to an end with many of the hotels and guest houses closed and the small pleasure steamers tarpaulined. A group of Japanese tourists wandered along the edge of the misty lake and, over on the tiny island in the middle of the water, even the black, flapping ravens were calling to one another cheerfully as if overjoyed that yet another busy summer charade had come to an end and they could now get their island, lake and all that cold water back to themselves. A heron pinned a desultory arc of beautiful flight right against the roof of the grey sky.

More than 14 million people now live within three hours' drive of the Lake District and, on some summer days, when the sun is high, it looks as if all 14 million of them have decided to turn up here at the same time. The joke went that they found a man lying full length in one gutter in the village of Grasmere and he explained that, as he had now found a parking space, he had sent his wife off to buy a car. Many of those tourists dig up the daffodils, knock over drystone walls or tramp across the fields. Crag rats or plastic pigs, the local farmers call them.

Grasmere, normally something of a flourishing tourist trading post, was quiet on the autumnal morning I got there and the massed armies of ghetto blasters and toffee apples had gone off to attack somewhere else. But there's still an inescapable rattiness about the place with its yellow parking lines and car parks and tacky tea rooms. I had a meal in one which only succeeded in making me feel ill and I later wandered around the lake trying to remember those great Wordsworthian lines that had been hammered into my indifferent brain as a schoolboy. 'One impulse from a hot-dog stall can teach us more of man . . .' 'My heart leaps up when I behold a bed and breakfast sign in the sky . . .' 'I wandered lonely as a parking ticket . . .'

From Wordsworth to de Quincey and Ruskin the Lakes have always attracted nutters, who have then charmingly and quietly gone around the bend. Wordsworth said that this watery landscape had actually formed him while his poetry was later to turn all these lakeland villages into places of pilgrimage: shrines to the Muse where we could still come and hope to experience God as Wordsworth experienced God in 'unknown modes of being' or listen to the 'still, sad music of humanity'.

Wordsworth saw God in the natural world and believed that this world was a vital, formative influence on us. Nature has a life and a force in its own right, he said; every flower actually enjoys the air it breathes. Nature also joins its power to the power of human mind and feeling; nature helps us to see into the 'life of things'.

Christian theologians tend to dismiss this pantheism airily but we do know that writers as diverse as Osbert Sitwell, Vladimir Nabokov, C. Day-Lewis and Julian Huxley all claimed to have received profound and often terrible mystical insights from the natural world.

Yet it would certainly be difficult to lay any modern claim to Dorothy Wordsworth's 'glorious wild solitude under that lofty purple crag' that her brother once found so inspirational since, in these parts at least, it is simply no longer there. Cramponed climbers swarm all over the crags destroying the flora and fauna and there are the litterers and the dopeheads and the motor cyclists roaring up the passes. Even Wordsworth's old home of

Dove Cottage in Grasmere is now a museum becalmed in a Sargasso sea of yellow lines.

But the inside is pleasant enough with a woman explaining that, somehow, Wordsworth with his wife and children all lived in here hugger-mugger with Samuel Coleridge and Thomas de Quincey. Apparently de Quincey had a serious drug problem since he needed a jug of laudanum (opium) a day to keep going and that old junky Coleridge needed half a gallon a week.

There are endless problems in Grasmere today, this woman added. Stones in the cottage's garden are constantly being stolen. There are always mighty rows in the village about development plans. Insensitively designed extensions are being tacked on to hotels, and old mullioned windows are being taken out. A nun was actually photographed digging up a flower right there in that garden.

I had been to the Lakes often enough before but this time had made my pilgrimage here in the autumn perhaps hoping to get a new handle on the place but, as it turned out, I again felt that I had come to nothing at all. The overall picture was all right and, particularly if you were up high in the peaks, you could still pick up something of Wordsworth's 'blended holiness of earth and sky'. But the day-to-day details of the place had gone seriously askew and were both disappointing and jarring. There was nothing on offer to the pilgrim at this pantheist shrine so I decided to leave almost quickly as I had arrived, venturing back out on to my shifting continents of falling leaves and morning dreams.

I heard it before I saw it; a steady hissing in a distant wood. Leaves crunched underfoot as I followed this hissing when I spotted a white slash in the yellow and gold leaves. By now the path had become extremely slippery and I had to step carefully as I approached this great white cascade which curved upwards slightly before tumbling straight down the face of a small cliff before smashing into a pool directly below.

Each waterfall is completely perfect in its own way; each is an exquisite and unimprovable poem of white light and dazzling movement. All waterfalls are making burly, angry sounds just now after so much rain and there are lots of dead tree branches and trunks lying across the rivers and streams.

But this one, up here in the north, would be especially pleasing for even the most veteran waterfall-spotter, tearing through a gap in the smooth stone before hurling itself with a suicidal abandon down on to the steaming rocks below.

Every waterfall has its own music from the merry tinklings of smaller waterfalls through to the louder chucklings of the larger ones and then on to the thrilling bass thunder of the great waterfalls, full of ancient defiance as they trumpet the spectacular news of the marriage between water and gravity. Yet this one had a light, tinkling voice with a background of percussive thunder. Deep within it was a vein of light laughter: the chortling happiness of a man telling a pleasing story.

The walk up the path beside it was difficult with the damp stones slipping away from beneath my unsteady feet. But after reaching the top I could follow the stream up the small gorge for a while, actually being able to hang on to the branch of a tree directly above the moving water from where I could look back to where it fell.

And as I hung there I thought of Butch Cassidy and the Sundance Kid, of the one shouting that he couldn't swim before they both leaped into that river down in that deep canyon. And as soon as I thought of those two I let go of the branch and got back on to dry ground fast. Those movies will ruin everything for us in the end; I've never much enjoyed swimming in the sea after seeing *Jaws*.

Just before the actual fall off the cliff the water seemed to slow and dawdle as if unsure if it wanted to jump or not. But then it picked up an accelerating speed as if under the crack of a whip before leaping into the air and crashing down in screaming banshees of the whitest fury. The purer the water, they say, the whiter the foam.

I've sat next to some really lovely waterfalls over the years and pondered on the meaning and nature of every one of them but this one was all I wanted and needed this northern morning. Perhaps you cannot actually see or feel God in nature, as the pantheists often insist they can, but I am sure you can often see his attributes and qualities in astonishing sculptures of light and movement like this. Every waterfall I've ever been near seems to sing its own song of purity and renewal; they also keep busily explaining the secrets of the land to us and you can also see, by the way the pools below are surrounded by trees, birds and lots of plants, that water remains the source of all life.

The constant toil and energy of waterfalls also tell us something about God, I think. They're without any form of blemish and seem prepared to trumpet away for all eternity.

And then, just when the summer looked as if she had fully and finally been lowered into the ground and the grave-diggers were busily piling earth and dead leaves on to her coffin and the people were ransacking their drawers and wardrobes for their winter woollies and it looked as if we were all in for weeks and months, if not years and centuries, of cold rain spitting straight at our miserable faces, then something big, somewhere important in the machinery of the planet threw everything into reverse gear and there was a large and brilliant resurrection of the spirit throughout the land with sunshine and warmth spiralling straight up out of that grave, all coming together to create a simply gorgeous Indian summer.

This was not such good news for everyone since the children had long gone back to school after their summer holidays and were left sitting in their airless classrooms with glowing windows, daydreaming of robbing banks or of life on a Californian beach. But otherwise everyone else and their dog were scuttling outdoors in all these mellow rills of sunshine, picking up fallen conkers in the parks or ploughing up the weeds in their allotments or trampling into blackberry bushes and reaching out for those hidden, fat bunches which had suddenly and unexpectedly been baked to perfection by this Indian summer sun.

On such days, with the seasons on a red and gold cusp and lovers stopping to kiss on the corners, with the old wino sitting in the shop doorway dressed, as ever, for the dead of winter and with the new autumn styles appearing in the shop windows and with the flies and wasps slowing up and falling dead on their backs on window sills with their little legs poking up into the air and with the soccer season already well underway with Newcastle United going straight to the top, you feel what a great pleasure it would be to walk the northern lanes forever.

You walk and look around you seeing this great and beautiful actress struggling to get up out of her rumpled and self-indulgent bed. The countryside will never look or feel quite so radiant as she does now; a fabulous star sitting at her dressing table and preparing herself for the rigours of winter as her full body was still warm and throbbing with the afterglow of summer.

So when she had finally finished preening herself at her dressing table you took her hand and continued walking along the lanes with her, the both of you basking in all these enthralling promises of new warmth and sunshine without end. And you clung to these promises blindly and you *believed* them implicitly even though you knew in your heart that all these promises were false promises and that soon, far sooner than ever you would have hoped for, everything was going to be snatched away from you only to disappear into long and bitter centuries of cold winds and freezing gusts of rain.

But not just yet; not today anyway since the Indian summer held on with the firmest of grips and I was chugging out of the Northumberland town of Seahouses in a launch to visit the Farne Islands in search of St Cuthbert, whose spirit once so gloriously illuminated these parts. The very swell of the waves seemed to have imprisoned the sunshine as we chugged on towards the stained cliffs of these volcanic islands where, on the furthest one, lots of seals in the Grey Seal colony began slipping off their ledges and disappearing into the water.

The boat engine was cut off and they kept bobbing up and looking at us with large, black, worried eyes. Seals like to sleep deep in the sea, going down vertically where they just hang there like overcoats in a vestry, before coming up every five minutes or so to take a breath. Otherwise they will just loll about on those rock ledges, waving their flippers around and gossiping with their mates. Their faeces have stained the black rocks like dried-up brown ice cream and the overwhelming stink which kept marauding out to us over the waves was of rotten fish.

The boat engine started up again, making a lot of those watchful eyes disappear in panic before we moved off to the Inner Farne, disembarking on a small, wooden jetty. Here we followed a rough stone path leading up to the tiny St Cuthbert's Chapel with its beheaded carvings of angels and oak choir stalls. There are also small cottages in this complex, for the National Trust wardens, and, over on the other side of the lichen and campion-dotted slopes, is a lighthouse.

Somewhere near this spot – although no one knows exactly where – Cuthbert built his beehive-shaped cell in 676, remaining here until his death in 684. Here he would have conducted his long, passionate hours of secret prayer amidst all these birds and then there would have been the long, cold nights in his cell with the winds howling at its walls and the seals singing their love songs from their stained ledges in the distance.

But the overwhelming feature of this small island is not a peaceful silence in which we might imagine that Cuthbert worshipped God but the huge and terrifying noise of the thousands of the nesting birds, not quite so raucous now that we were at the end of the season although a lot of them were still at it even though such as the puffin, tern and guillemot had already gone off to make their rackets elsewhere. The guillemots, in particular, stage fantastic displays of collective flight in the season, taking off from the edges of the Pinnacle Rocks right over there at the first sight of a boat and fluttering around in a huge circle before coming back to land again, the first bird arriving back just as the last bird was taking off.

It is a very big mistake to think of birds as being sweet and kind to one another since this whole island is often the sad witness to scenes of necrophilia, mob attacks, murder, incessant fighting with the neighbours or else eating each other's baby young. Birds haven't the slightest clue how to live together with any sense of Christian amity and one of the National Trust wardens here like Alex Chown will all too happily explain, in long and lurid detail, how the herring gulls will eat the baby puffins; how the guillemots are always brawling with their neighbours; how fulmars will spit four-inch long spurts of black oil at any intruders and how the small feisty terns will attack anyone and anything stupid enough to go near their eggs.

How then, I wondered, could someone like Cuthbert have lived here amongst this unreconstructed rabble? Well, he would have found it very difficult, Alex thought. Keeping the drinking water free from contamination might have been the biggest problem since the faeces of just one puffin would be enough to poison one whole barrel. Those faeces would also stain the clothes and skin, as the National Trust wardens knew all too well.

Then Cuthbert would have needed to have grown vegetables and the greedy rabbits would also have been after them while the terns in particular are likely to have nested in his carrots and then fought anyone who tried to pull them. There would also have been the mighty northerly winds to deal with in the winter and those seas ripping through blow holes up to a hundred feet in height. All in all, Alex decided, life here would have been hell for old Cuthbert.

So we might already be coming to an understanding of this northern saint; a singular man with thermal-lined bones and a belly of the purest iron. It is possible that he escaped the full brunt of those North Sea blasts by building his cell with thick walls. We do know that he made the cell floor very deep so that he could keep his mind on 'heavenly things'. An unusual adage this: when you want to think high go deep. It's normally the other way around.

Writers like the estimable David Adam of Lindisfarne believe that Cuthbert probably reached some sort of accommodation with the unruly birds here on Inner Farne although it is perhaps significant that Cuthbert did have a special relationship with the one sweet-natured and agreeable bird around these parts, the eider duck – or Cuddy's Ducks as they came to be known – who are so placid that you can even put your hands underneath them as they sit on their nests and then count their eggs.

So I just stood there on that bird-loud headland on that Indian summer afternoon, looking out at the waves washing the rocks, trying to picture Cuthbert with his strange and saintly rapport with birds and the way he often liked to stand in the sea all night praising God when, in the morning, or so the story went, the seals came over to him, drying and warming him with their breath.

All at once Cuthbert's whole shadow seemed to rise up out of the sunlight and hover up and over me and I found myself falling backwards with my hands windmilling around and my eyes widening in a spasm of fear. 'Better get a move on,' this menacing shadow from the National Trust said. 'The boat will be leaving in five minutes.'

Warm winds gusted against my cheeks as I stood on the thin metalled causeway in the middle of nowhere watching two cormorants coming down to land on the sands where they were now standing with their wings stretched apart like feathery crosses and drying themselves in the same warm winds. Further out again a herring gull was flapping its wings but going nowhere and, further out again, a dread of small birds kept wheeling around and around in the huge mackerel skies.

I was standing on the causeway to Lindisfarne – or Holy Island as it is otherwise known – just near to one of the high refuge boxes into which you have to clamber if you are caught by the tide and have to call for help as your car floats away. The flat sands all around were massive with their own emptiness with only the odd pools catching the light as small crabs moved through them black on silver. Just near this road was a line of rough poles stretching across the sands, marking the route of Pilgrims' Way where bare-footed pilgrims carry a huge cross over to the island every Easter.

Lindisfarne becomes an island again twice a day when the tides come swarming in over the sands and drown this causeway. Then everything seems to stop for a while with nothing moving except the sea and the call of the sandpiper. When Christ steps back on to the stage of the world it will surely be somewhere like this; not to a fanfare of trumpets in a gaudy coronation coach but on his own, with a staff and barefoot, following a line of rough wooden poles and to the welcoming fanfare of a couple of stray sandpipers.

The small island village is quiet just now, licking its wounds and counting its money after an exceptionally busy summer season and getting ready for the usual seasonal rites of the Harvest Festival with gladioli and fruit and vegetables in the spruce, trim church. With a population of just 150 the village is a small collection of stone cottages standing around a sort of square and the traditional broken priory ruin standing about in the traditional broken manner. Soon it will be Guy Fawkes' night and they will be burning him all over again.

But, even on such a small island, there are still secret places where you can repair and sit with yourself watching the small boats in the tropical-shaped lagoon or the strangely geometric upturned shapes of the fishing huts or the reconstructed castle clinging to the rocky summit of a crag – the highest point on the island – or the huge wooden cross on top of that steep bank.

There really is a sense of spirituality about this island which comes throbbing up out of the ground as surely as if it was being made by some sort of angelic generator. This power can enfold and hold you as you sit in your secret place; it can give you a sense of hope and enormous possibilities; it can tell you that here indeed is a place to make a fresh start where nothing, as yet, is wrong or indeed about to go wrong. Here indeed is a place to dwell in the tides of men; here is an island, they say, with walls so thin that you really can reach out and lay your trembling fingertips on the very mind and heart of God.

This blinding optimism is all here somehow, factored straight into all that thrumming spirituality. It's also out there in the boats moored on the pebbles; in the outline of the clinging castle and hang-gliding in the drifting holiness of all those sea breezes. I've never once been here without feeling pure hope and real optimism; never looked around me in my secret place without picking up a gusting sense of the resurrection. All you need to do is just sit here and let it all work over you.

These feelings are so real you also know that you can, if you want, reach out and take hold of St Cuthbert's hand since he once ruled and lived here before going to the Farnes, followed around by his ducks while also being sought out by the sick or merely fed-up from the mainland. He once healed a woman's dying baby with a kiss and it was here also that he first received the call to become a hermit on the Farnes.

Yes, dear, sweet Cuthbert is here with us all still, commanded to haunt the island and her tides and winds until the end of time.

When I began this pilgrimage in those Cornish lanes at the beginning of the summer I set out to try and find out something about the spiritual state of contemporary England. I have not come close to working that out but I have found, from the evidence of my own eyes, that, contrary to what is often supposed, we generally remain a faithful people, fond of the practice of prayer and trusting in God's future good plans for us.

Even sitting here now in Lindisfarne I can go fly-spinning in the rivers of my memory and haul in pictures of those praying and faithful monks in Buckfast and Prinknash; the impeccable condition of the dozens of churches I have knelt in and all those abbeys and islands which are kept afloat by long hours of believing prayer. And then there were all those soaring stone cathedrals and those vast worshipping slopes at the Greenbelt communion service. Other images come back to me too; Walsingham in the rain and the wind-ravaged Yorkshire Moors. Then there were the pilgrim moments on Dartmoor and the freezing presence of Etheldreda in Ely. Let's not forget those dreams of attacking lions too.

All these pictures come crowding in together in my consciousness telling me that, in a sense, the whole country is one vast web of secret prayer; a web which is not public because the whole point of prayer is that it is a solitary and private activity; it is by its very nature secret.

If God does decide on the return of the Son of Man and if the whole army of angels is mobilizing at this very minute and if this return was to take place somewhere secret and holy like this spot in Lindisfarne then, yes, a huge part of the country would be prepared and ready. Yes, there are untold thousands of secret places of prayer and a large number of people who would not be taken by surprise since they are still waiting patiently and faithfully, in a permanent state of readiness and preparedness, all holding up the glittering candles of their living faith in the encroaching darkness.

That's about what I did find out in my summer pilgrimage through England. The skies keep darkening but we remain faithful still.

The weather forecast on the radio said that our gorgeous Indian summer will end in cold rain showers in a couple of days so I am going home to my family in Wales. There was the unfamiliar chatter of a bird over near the castle and a distant screech of female laughter. Water was washing softly against the rocks and the sun was soon going to dip out of the sky. House lights were going on in the village and there was the throaty sound of a tractor.

There are never ends to journeys any more than there are ever ends of pilgrimages. Our journeys and pilgrimages always keep going as we struggle through one to start another, only knowing for certain that there will be another one and another one after that. But, with every pilgrimage across strange and often savage landscapes, we also know that we are somehow coming closer to God's heart and purpose; with every step we are coming to a clearer understanding that his eyes are filled with tears just like ours.

We pilgrims are also coming to understand that no one – not even God – can live imprisoned in such sadness for a lot longer. We are beginning to suspect that these really are the promised end times of lawlessness and that he will make a move soon and send back the son he loves so much if only because he has run out of options. For a lot of us this suspicion is becoming knowledge. We really are beginning to see the shape of a huge ship of faith which is soon going to be launched on the polluted tides of the world. So hold on my people, hold on.

It would be nice to say that I saw a rainbow at that moment. But I didn't. All I saw was a darkness crowding in over the island

107

and I began chattering with cold. So I simply brought my summer pilgrimage to an end by standing up on that holy shoreline, waving my tatty pilgrim flag and spouting a little more ruined poetry in front of a large cross in a dying Lindisfarne sun.

Also available from
Triangle

Books by David Adam

THE OPEN GATE
Celtic prayers for growing spiritually

A rich mine of resources both for personal daily prayer and
corporate weekly worship.

THE EDGE OF GLORY
Prayers in the Celtic tradition

Prayers recapturing the Celtic way of intertwining divine glory
with everyday events.

THE CRY OF THE DEER
Meditations on the hymn of St Patrick

Meditations leading to practical exercises which take us deeper
into the prayer experience in affirming the presence of God.

TIDES AND SEASONS
Modern prayers in the Celtic tradition

Prayers which echo the rhythms of creation, finding their
parallels in our spiritual lives and in the highs and lows of all
human experience.

THE EYE OF THE EAGLE
Meditations on the hymn 'Be Thou My Vision'

A series of meditations on a favourite hymn, uncovering its
spiritual riches.

POWER LINES
Celtic prayers about work

Modern prayers about our day by day work, incorporating the
insights of the Celtic tradition.

Also available from
Triangle

THE POST-EVANGELICAL
by Dave Tomlinson

A controversial book which should be read by every person
disaffected by their experience of evangelicalism – and by
every evangelical leader. It raises vital pastoral and theological
issues, within a biblically-based framework, and highlights the
agenda facing Christians at the close of the twentieth century.

BREAD OF LIFE
Stories of Radical Mission

Ronald Sider tells the stories of ten ministries around the
world that combine social action and evangelism in a radical
agenda, bringing Kingdom values into the lives of ordinary
people. Included are the stories behind Steve Chalke's Oasis
Trust, and Roger and Faith Forster and the Ichthus Fellowship.

MEMBERS ONLY?
Is the church becoming too exclusive?

This entertaining and revealing book gives a unique glimpse of
the Church of England. Backed up by a specially commissioned
survey, former BBC Religious Affairs Correspondent
Ted Harrison looks at the *real* attitudes of clergy and people
towards the vital question of whether the church has become
no more than an exclusive club, no longer providing ministry
for all.

TRIANGLE
Books
can be obtained from all good bookshops.

In case of difficulty, or for a complete list of our books, contact:
SPCK Mail Order
36 Steep Hill
Lincoln
LN2 lLU
(tel: 01522 527486)

Or dial O345 626747 (local rate)